Classic Learning Test Quantitative Reasoning Practice Exams with Tips and CLT Math Review Study Guide

Classic Learning Test Quantitative Reasoning Practice Exams with Tips and CLT Math Review Study Guide

ISBN: 978-1-949282-87-0

Note: The Classic Learning Test and CLT Exam are registered trademarks of Classic Learning Initiatives, LLC, which is neither affiliated with nor endorses this publication.

HOW TO USE THIS PUBLICATION

There are five complete CLT practice math tests for you to study in this book, for a total of 200 exam problems in the study guide.

If you feel like you need to review your math skills before taking the first practice test, you should start by completing the math review questions in practice test 5. Then proceed to the remaining tests in the book.

You will find the all of the math formulas needed for the exam at the front of the book. In practice test 1, you will see examples of how to use each the math exam formulas, as well as exam tips and test-taking strategies.

You may wish to refer back to the formulas and explanations in the first section of the study guide, as well as the formula sheet, as you complete the remaining practice tests in the book.

Note that the drawings in this publication are not necessarily to scale.

You may also be interested in our other publication:

Classic Learning Test Prep with CLT Verbal Reasoning and Grammar/Writing Practice Exams

TABLE OF CONTENTS

Classic Learning Test Practice Math Exam 1

Mathematics Formula Sheet

SECTION 1

You should know the formulas in this section from memory. They will not be given in the math formulas provided with your exam.

Midpoint formula
$(x_1 + x_2) \div 2$, $(y_1 + y_2) \div 2$

Point-slope formula
$y - y_1 = m(x - x_1)$

Slope formula
rise/run $= y_2 - y_1/x_2 - x_1$

Slope-intercept formula
$y = mx + b$
m is the slope of the line and b is the y-intercept

x and y intercepts
$y = 0$ for the x intercept
$x = 0$ for the y intercept

Quadratic formula
$$x = \frac{-b \pm \sqrt{b^2 - 4ac}}{2a}$$

Factorials
Multiply the number before the exclamation point by every non-zero integer less than that number.
Example: $5! = 5 \times 4 \times 3 \times 2 \times 1$

Combinations
$N! \div [S!(N - S)!]$ where N equals the number of items in the set and S equals the selection size

Mean (arithmetic average)
To find the mean, add up all of the items in the set and then divide by the number of items in the set. Consider the data set 5, 2, 4, 1, 3. There are 5 numbers in the set. Add them together and divide by 5:
$(5 + 2 + 4 + 1 + 3) \div 5 = 3$

Median
Consider the data set 5, 2, 4, 1, 3
Put the numbers in ascending order:
5, 4, **3**, 2, 1
Find the one that is in the middle: 3

Mode
The mode is the number that occurs the most frequently in the set.
Consider the data set 5, 5, 2, 4, 1, 3
The mode is 5 because it occurs twice, but the other numbers only occur once.

Range
High value minus low value
Consider the data set 5, 2, 4, 1, 3
Range: $5 - 1 = 4$

Probability
Probability $= E \div S$; E is the event or the number of items available for the desired outcome; S is the sample space or the total number of items available in the set.

Example: In a standard deck of playing cards, what is the chance of drawing a diamond?

Answer: There are 52 cards in a standard deck of cards. This is the sample space. There are 13 diamonds in a standard deck of cards. This is the event.
Probability $= 13 \div 52 = \frac{1}{4}$

Rectangle
perimeter $= 2(length + width)$

Rectangular Solid (Box)
volume $= length \times width \times height$

Cube
volume $= (length\ of\ side)^3$

Cylinder
volume $= \pi \times (radius)^2 \times height$

Pythagorean triples

The rule of Pythagorean triples states that the three sides of a right-angled triangle can be expressed in the form $a^2 + b^2 = c^2$, with a, b, and c all being integers that are expressed in the ratio: $a: b: c$.

Some examples of Pythagorean triples are as follows:
3: 4: 5
6: 8: 10
5: 12: 13
7: 24: 25

Radians

The following formulas can be used for calculations with radians, where θ = the radians of the subtended angle, s = arc length, and r = radius:
$\theta = s \div r$
$s = r\,\theta$
Also remember these useful formulas.
$\pi \times 2 \times \text{radians} = 360°$
$\pi \times \text{radians} = 180°$
$\pi \div 2 \times \text{radians} = 90°$
$\pi \div 4 \times \text{radians} = 45°$
$\pi \div 6 \times \text{radians} = 30°$

Sine and cosine

Be sure that you are well acquainted with the rules for sine and cosine that follow:

$\sin\left(\frac{\pi}{2}\right) = 1 \qquad \cos\left(\frac{\pi}{2}\right) = 0$

$\sin\left(\frac{\pi}{4}\right) = \frac{\sqrt{2}}{2} \qquad \cos\left(\frac{\pi}{4}\right) = \frac{\sqrt{2}}{2}$

$\sin\left(\frac{\pi}{6}\right) = \frac{1}{6} \qquad \cos\left(\frac{\pi}{6}\right) = \frac{\sqrt{3}}{2}$

Sine function

The period of the sine function is 2π.

SECTION 2

The formulas in this section will be provided for you during the exam.

Circle

(Use 3.14 for the value of π when required)
circumference = $\pi \times diameter$
area = $\pi \times (radius)^2$
There are 360° in a circle.
There are 2π radians in a circle.

Triangle

area = ½ ($base \times height$)
sum of angles = 180°

Pythagorean Theorem

$C = \sqrt{A^2 + B^2}$

Rectangle

area = $length \times width$

Sphere (Ball)

volume = $\frac{4}{3} \times \pi \times \text{radius}^3$
surface area = $4\pi r^2$

Trigonometry:

sin θ = opposite/hypotenuse
cos θ = adjacent/hypotenuse
tan θ = opposite/adjacent
csc θ = 1/sin θ
sec θ = 1/cos θ
cot θ = 1/tan θ
tan θ = sin θ/cos θ
$\sin^2\theta + \cos^2\theta = 1$
The lengths of the sides of 30°–60°–90° triangles are in a ratio of 1: $\sqrt{3}$: 2.
The side lengths of a 45°–45°–90° triangle are in a ratio of 1: 1: $\sqrt{2}$.

Classic Learning Test Practice Math Exam 1

Instructions: If you feel that you need to review any of the algebraic, geometric, or trigonometric concepts covered on the CLT math exam, you may wish to complete the 40 algebra, geometry, and trigonometry review questions in practice exam 5 of the book before attempting the other practice tests. Practice test 1 is written in study guide format, with exam tips and hints after each question. Take your time completing practice test 1 to be sure you understand how best to answer each question. To simulate exam conditions, you should then attempt to complete all 40 questions in each of the remaining practice tests in 45 minutes. The answers and explanations for all of the problems are provided at the back of the book.

1. Consider a set of integers between 125 and 225 inclusive. How many integers will satisfy both of the following conditions?
   1: The integer is 25 more than a perfect square.
   2: The integer contains two even digits and one odd digit.
   A) 2
   B) 3
   C) 5
   D) 6

   > Tip: A perfect square is an integer to the power of 2. In other words, it is an integer multiplied by itself. So, 4 is a perfect square because $2 \times 2 = 4$. To solve, find the perfect squares between 100 and 200 and add 25 to each one. Then see how many of these satisfy condition 2.

2. If Ð is a special operation defined by $(x \, Ð \, y) = (30x \div 9y)$ and $(3 \, Ð \, y) = 10$, then $y = ?$
   A) 1
   B) 3
   C) 9
   D) 30

   > Tip: We have the special operation defined as $(x \, Ð \, y) = (30x \div 9y)$. Looking at the relationship between the left-hand side and the right-hand side of this equation, we can determine the operations that need to be performed on any new equation containing the operation Ð and variables x and y. For our problem, the new equation will be carried out as follows: Operation Ð is division; the number or variable before the special operation symbol is multiplied by 30; and the number or variable after the special operation symbol is multiplied by 9.

3. Which quadratic below has a double root?
   A) $y = x^2 - 12$
   B) $y = x^2 + 12x + 144$
   C) $y = x^2 + 24x + 144$
   D) $y = 2x^2 + 24x + 144$

   > Tip: A quadratic equation may be expressed in the form $0 = ax^2 + bx + c$. To find the double root of a quadratic you must factor the quadratic, and the terms inside each set of parentheses must be identical. For instance, $(x + y)(x + y)$.

4. Susan goes to a store to purchase a plastic storage container and determines that three possible sizes might suits her needs. (Note that all measurements below are provided in inches.)
Box L: $24 \times 16 \times 10$
Box M: $28 \times 18 \times 12$
Box N: $35 \times 25 \times 15$
Susan is trying to fit eight shoe boxes inside the storage container. The shoes boxes are identical and measure $13 \times 5 \times 8$ each. If Susan wants to purchase only one container for all eight shoe boxes, then which one of the above will leave the least empty space in the container after the shoe boxes have been placed in it?
A) Box L
B) Box M
C) Box N
D) Either Box M or Box N

Tip: For these questions, consider whether the items could be placed inside the container horizontally, vertically, diagonally, or front to back. You may find it helpful to draw 3-D diagrams for each of the containers and work out how the items can be placed inside each one. Look at the example diagram below if you need further help to answer this question.

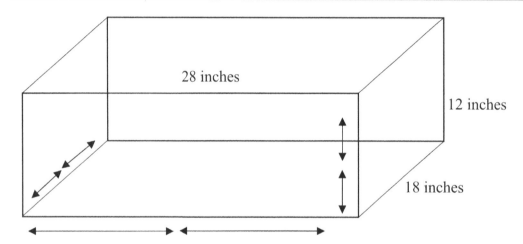

5. Consider the following facts: $x = 6$, $g(x) = 2x + 4$ and $f(g(x)) = 23$. Which of the following could represent $f(x)$?
A) $x + 29$
B) $x + 16$
C) $x + 6$
D) $x + 7$

Tip: This is a question on functions. A function will yield an output, also called the range, for a series of inputted values, also called the domain. Substitute 6 for the value of x in the function $g(x)$. Then use inverse operations with this value to determine $f(x)$.

6. x and y are integers, and $x - y$ is a negative even integer. Which of the following must be true?
A) $x + y$ is a positive integer.
B) $x \times y$ is an even integer.
C) x and y are both odd integers.
D) None of the above.

Tip: Be sure that you know the properties of integers for the exam.

Addition: (1) Even + Even = Even; (2) Odd + Odd = Even; (3) Even + Odd = Odd;
(4) Odd + Even = Odd

Subtraction: (1) Even − Even = Even; (2) Odd − Odd = Even; (3) Even − Odd = Odd;
(4) Odd − Even = Odd

Multiplication: (1) Even × Even = Even; (2) Odd × Odd = Odd; (3) Even × Odd = Even;
(4) Odd × Even = Even

Division: (1) Even ÷ Even = Even or Odd; (2) Odd ÷ Odd = Odd; (3) Even ÷ Odd = Even;
(4) Odd ÷ Even: does not result in an integer

7. In triangle XYZ below, $\overline{XY} = \overline{XZ}$, and $\overline{YZ} = 6$ inches. When an altitude is drawn in the triangle, the resulting measurement of the altitude is 1 more than three times the length of $\overline{YZ}$. What is the length in inches of side $\overline{XY}$?

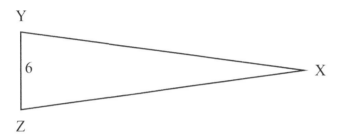

A) 19
B) $\sqrt{109}$
C) $\sqrt{370}$
D) $\sqrt{397}$

Tip: This is an isosceles triangle since it has two equal sides. An altitude is a perpendicular line drawn from the apex of the triangle to the base. Determine the length of the altitude from the facts stated in the problem, and then use the Pythagorean Theorem to solve: $C = \sqrt{A^2 + B^2}$

8. Find the equivalent of the following: $\left(\dfrac{6a^2}{3a^{-6}}\right)^3$
    A) $2a^{12}$
    B) $2a^{24}$
    C) $8a^{24}$
    D) $2a^8$

Tip: Be sure to remember the following exponent laws for the exam. When you have a shared base variable, such as a in the problem above, you need to subtract the exponents when performing division. So, $x^5 \div x^2 = x^3$. However, you need to add the exponents when doing multiplication. So, $x^5 \times x^2 = x^7$. When an exponent is outside another variable that already has an exponent, you need to multiply exponents. So, $(x^3)^3 = x^9$

9. Which of the following could NOT be a value of x, if $20 > |4x - 2|$?
    A) −5
    B) 1/2
    C) 2
    D) 3

> Tip: When you see algebraic expressions inside lines like this, you are being asked the absolute value. To find the absolute value of any number or expression, you take the result of the expression inside the lines and express it as a positive number, so for example $|-2| = 2$

10. Five amps is equal to 600 watts on an electrical current of 120 volts. Electricians have discovered that one particular current of 120 volts is at 7.5 amp. How many watts does it have?
    A) 600
    B) 900
    C) 120
    D) 16

> Tip: For questions on proportions like this one, find the value of one unit first of all. Here we are being asked about watts, so determine how many watts are equivalent to one amp as your first step towards solving the problem.

11. Which one of the following is equivalent to $\sin^2 x + 3 + \cos^2 x$?
    A) 2
    B) 3
    C) $^3/\sin^2 x$
    D) 4

> Tip: Look at the trigonometric formulas on the math formula sheet. If you rearrange the variables in the above expression, one of the trigonometric formulas will help you solve the problem.

12. In the xy-plane, line B passes through the origin and is perpendicular to line A. Line A passes through the points (2, −5) and (6, 3). The equation of line B could be which one of the following?
    A) $y = 2x + 0$

    B) $y = \frac{1}{2}x + 0$

    C) $y = -\frac{1}{2}x + 0$

    D) $y = -2x + 0$

> Tip: To solve questions on perpendicular lines like this one, you first need to find the slope of the line provided in the question. The slopes of perpendicular lines are negative reciprocals of each other. So, to get the negative reciprocal of line A, you first need to invert the integer to make a fraction and then make that fraction negative.

13. You are inviting Tom, Maria, Paul, Sue, and Jeri to your house for a meal. Tom won't sit next to Paul, and Paul won't sit next to Maria. Jeri has to sit next to Sue. You have a circular table for you and your five guests. Which of the following is a suitable seating plan?
    A) Tom, Maria, Paul, Sue, Jeri, You
    B) Tom, Paul, Sue, Jeri, You, Maria
    C) Paul, Sue, Jeri, Tom, Maria, You
    D) Paul, Sue, Maria, Jeri, Tom, You

> Tip: For logical reasoning questions like this one, try to rule out each of the answer choices one-by-one by seeing whether they violate any of the conditions that are stated in the facts of the problem.

14. The orbits around the earth of particular two satellites, called *S* and *T*, are circular. Satellite *S* is at an altitude of approximately 42,178 kilometers from the center of the earth, while the altitude of satellite *T* is 12,647 less than this. In a single orbit, satellite *S* travels approximately 264,878 kilometers. If takes each satellite 24 hours to orbit the earth, what is the approximate difference in speed between the two satellites? Use 3.14 for π.
    A) Satellite *S* travels 3,310 km per hour faster than satellite *T*.
    B) Satellite *S* travels 3,310 km per hour slower than satellite *T*.
    C) Satellite *S* travels 6,519 km per hour faster than satellite *T*.
    D) Satellite *S* travels 6,519 km per hour slower than satellite *T*.

> Tip: This is essentially a question on circumference, with the each of the paths of the orbits representing a circumference around the earth. Use the formula for circumference to find the distance traveled for each satellite: radius × 2 × 3.14 ≈ circumference. Then calculate the kilometers per hour for each satellite to solve: km travelled ÷ 24 hours = km per hour

15. Find the equivalent: $\dfrac{\cot A}{\tan A \times \csc A}$

    A) $\tan A / \cos A$

    C) $\cos A \times \tan A$

    B) $\cos A / \tan A$

    D) $\csc A$

> Tip: These types of problems can look extremely difficult at first, but they are simply substitution problems. Substitute the values from the trigonometric identities on the formula sheet for cot A, tan A, and csc A to solve.

16. A circle on the *xy*-coordinate plane is represented by the equation $(x - 5)^2 + (y - 4)^2$. The circle is rotated 90° clockwise about its center, and then this result is reflected across the *y*-axis. What are the coordinates of the center of this new circle?
    A) $(-5, 4)$
    B) $(-5, -4)$
    C) $(5, -4)$
    D) $(5, 4)$

> Tip: On the *xy*-coordinate plane, the equation for a circle is $(x - h)^2 + (y - k)^2$. For the center of the circle, the result of operations inside each set of parentheses is equal to zero.

17. A shampoo manufacturer combines 56 ml of 25% sodium lauryl sulfate with 32 ml of 40% sodium lauryl sulfate. What percentage best represents the strength of sodium lauryl sulfate in the combined solution?
    A) 22.5%
    B) 26.8%
    C) 30.45%
    D) 48.0%

> Tip: First find the volume of the new solution. Then determine the relative strength of each solution before they are combined. Finally, divide the sum of the relative percentages by the new volume to solve.

18. Circle Q lies on the xy-coordinate plane and is centered at the origin at point c. Point a has the coordinates $\left(\frac{\sqrt{3}}{2}, \frac{1}{2}\right)$ and point b has the coordinates $\left(\frac{\sqrt{3}}{2}, 0\right)$. Point b lies at the third vertex of triangle abc. Determine the angle measurements of triangle abc.
    A) 30°–60°–90°
    B) 45°–45°–90°
    C) 50°–40°–90°
    D) Cannot be determined.

> Tip: When you see that one of the coordinates contains a square root in the numerator or denominator, you should look at the rules for 30°– 60°– 90° and 45°– 45°–90° triangles on the formula sheet. When you have determined which type of triangle you are dealing with, use the rules of similarity to solve. The rules of similarity state that: (1) Two triangles are similar if two of their corresponding angles are congruent; or (2) Two triangles are similar if all three corresponding sides are in proportion; or (3) Two triangles are similar if 2 of their corresponding sides are in proportion and the angle in between them is congruent.

19. Consider the function $f(x) = \sqrt{x^3}$. Which of the following statements must be false with regard to real number values of this function?
    A) Its domain is all non-negative values of x.
    B) The function is represented on the xy-plane as a parabola.
    C) The smallest value of y for the function exists when $x = 0$.
    D) The range of the function consists of positive and negative integers.

> Tip: Check each statement by using example values. Remember that the domain consists of the possible inputs for a function, and the range consists of the possible outputs for the function.

20. If he were to do the work by himself, it would take a parent 20 hours to clean and organize the garage at their house. If the daughter were to do the job alone, it would take her 24 hours, while the teenage son, working alone, could to the job in 30 hours. If all three family members work together, how many hours will it take them to clean and organize the garage?
    A) 8
    B) 15
    C) 24
    D) 24²/₃

© COPYRIGHT 2023. Test Prep Guides dba www.test-prep-guides.com
This material may not be copied or reproduced in any form.

21. Vertex V is the vertex of an angle at the center of a circle. The diameter of the circle is 3. If the angle measures 60 degrees, what is the arc length relating to the central angle?

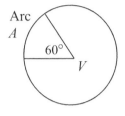

A) $\pi/2$

B) $\pi/4$

C) 2π

D) 4π

22. An owner of a carnival attraction draws teddy bears out of a bag at random to give to prize winners. She has 10 brown teddy bears, 8 white teddy bears, 4 black teddy bears, and 2 pink teddy bears when she opens the attraction at the start of the day. The first prize winner of the day receives a brown teddy bear. Which fraction below represents the likelihood of the second prize winner receiving a pink teddy bear?

A) $1/24$

B) $1/23$

C) $2/24$

D) $2/23$

23. The areas of two identical right-angled triangles add up to 60 square inches in total for both triangles. The perimeters of the two triangles also add up to 60 square inches. The shortest side of each of the triangles forms the base. What is the base length in inches of these two triangles?
    A) 5
    B) 10
    C) 12
    D) 13

> Tip: Be sure that you are acquainted with Pythagorean triples for the exam. We know that the rule of triples applies because the sums of both the perimeters and areas are even numbers, rather than numbers with radicals. Refer to the formula sheet if needed.

24. An ice cream store is offering a promotion of two free toppings on each sundae purchased. The store has the following toppings: chocolate chips, multi-colored sprinkles, marshmallows, toffee sauce, and strawberry sauce. How many 2-item combinations can be made from these ingredients? Note that two different ingredients must be selected.
    A) 5
    B) 10
    C) 15
    D) 20

> To determine the number of combinations of S at a time that can be made from a set containing N items, you need this formula: $(N!) \div [(N - S)! \times S!]$. In our problem, $S = 2$ and $N = 5$ (because there are five toppings available). When you see the exclamation mark, you need to take the number before the exclamation mark and multiply it by every positive integer less than it.

25. The figure shown below consists of five equal squares. The perimeter of the entire figure is 108 feet. What is the area the entire figure in square feet?

    A) 45
    B) 81
    C) 324
    D) 405

> Tip: Three sides of each of the exterior squares form the cross, so the cross has twelve sides. Get the length of one side of each square first. Then find the area of each square. Then multiply by the number of squares that make up the figure.

26. Find the solution to the system of equations that follow:
    $$\sqrt{b} + c = 2a$$
    $$c \times {}^a/_b = 10$$
    $$2b = 3a - c + 1$$
    A) (6, 16, 5)
    B) (5, 4, 8)

C) (2, 4, 5)
D) (4, 5, 1)

> Tip: If you are provided with possible solutions for systems of equations problems like this one, it is usually fastest to substitute the answer choices to see which one is correct, instead of trying to isolate variables in each equation. So, plug the numbers from the answer choices into the equations to see which answer works.

27. The central angle in the circle below is 90° and is subtended by an arc which is 8π centimeters in length. How many centimeters long is the radius of this circle?

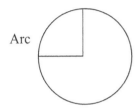

Arc

   A) 32
   B) 16
   C) 8π
   D) 8

> When working with arcs, you can calculate the radius or diameter of a circle if you have the measurement of a central angle and the length of the arc subtending the central angle. You will also need the formula for circumference: Circumference = π × radius × 2.

28. Which of the following equations is equivalent to $\frac{x}{5} < -\frac{y}{2} + x$?

   A) $x < \frac{x + y}{7}$

   B) $x > \frac{2x + 5y}{10}$

   C) $x > \frac{5x + 2y}{10}$

   D) $x < \frac{2x + 5y}{10}$

> Tip: When working with inequalities, get x on one side of the inequality to simplify. If the inequality has fractions, find the lowest common denominator. Remember that if you multiply by a negative number in an inequality problem, you need to reverse the direction that the sign points.

29. One-hundred students from Prep School Z apply for admission to two colleges, College X and College Y. The graduating class of the prep school consists of 100 students per year, and all 100 students apply to both colleges without applying elsewhere. Students can accept admission to only one of these colleges, and will always attend the college to which they have been admitted. In the previous academic year, college X admitted 54% of these students. College Y admitted 50% more of the graduating class in the current academic year than it did the previous academic year. According to these facts, which statements below must be true?

- (1) College X admitted 46 Prep School Z students in the current academic year.
- (2) College Y admitted more than 50% of the 100 Prep School Z students in the current academic year.
- (3) 23 more Prep School Z students attended College Y in in the current academic year than in the previous academic year.

   A) 1 only
   B) 2 only
   C) 2 and 3 only
   D) All of the above are true.

> Tip: It may be beneficial to make a table to keep track of the percentages for problems like this one. Put colleges X and Y in the rows, and the percentage attendance each academic year in the columns. If college X admitted 54% of the students (or 54 students) in the previous academic year, then how many students did college Y admit the previous year?

30. A tennis ball falls 200 feet from the balcony of a high-rise apartment. The tennis ball bounces a fourth as high as this after it hits the ground the first time. It then travels a fourth as high on each successive bounce as it has on the previous bounce. How many times does the ball have to bounce in order to travel a total distance 335 feet?
   A) More than 5 times
   B) 5 times
   C) 4 times
   D) 3 times

> Tip: Don't forget to count the distance the ball travels before it hits the ground the first time. Then consider how high it will bounce before falling the same distance as that bounce, and so on.

31. a^2 is a positive odd integer, and $a^b = 1$. If ab^{-2} is a real whole positive number, then ab^{-2} is equal to:
   A) $1/ab^2$
   B) b^2
   C) 1
   D) 0

> Tip: Problems like this one involve using multiple skills. Refer back to the rules on exponents and the laws of integers in the previous questions if needed.

32. The area of the base of a metal rectangular shipping crate is 40 square feet, and its length is 3 feet more than its width. The volume of the crate is 720 cubic feet. What is the height of the crate?
A) 5
B) 8
C) 12
D) 18

Tip: Questions like this one involve reverse calculations. This means that you are given the area or volume of a figure, for example, and you have to work backwards to find the missing length, width, height, or base. In this question, the length is 3 more than the width, so we can express the length as $x + 3$. We know that the area is 40, so calculate the length and height by working backwards.

33. A customer who owns a small hotel has ordered 10 new quilts. Each quilt requires 2 yards of red fabric for the front, 1 yard of blue fabric for the front, and a further 3 yards of blue fabric for the back. The quilts need to have an embellishment in gold, and a total amount of 12 yards of gold fabric is needed to make the embellishments for all 10 quilts. Each quilt also has edging in white, and half a yard of white material is needed for the edging for each quilt. What percentage of the total order of the fabric for these quilts will be red?
A) 10.81%
B) 11.11%
C) 25.97 %
D) 27.58%

Tip: Determine the total amount of material needed for all 10 quilts by adding up the totals for each individual color. To solve, find the total amount of the red material, and express the red material as a percentage of the material needed for the entire order.

34. What is the constant of the following sequence?

$$\frac{3}{10}, -\frac{1}{10}, \frac{1}{30}, \ldots$$

A) −30

B) −3

C) $-\frac{1}{3}$

D) 3

Tip: In order to create a geometric sequence, each number must be multiplied by a constant in order to get the subsequent number in the series. So, find the answer for c in the following equation order to solve: $\frac{3}{10} \times c = -\frac{1}{10}$

35. Triangle ABC and triangle XYZ are shown in the illustration below. ∠A is congruent to ∠X and $\overline{AB} = \overline{XY}$. Which of the following must also be true for triangles ABC and XYZ to be congruent? (Note that the drawing is not necessarily to scale.)

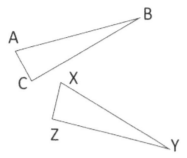

A) ∠B = ∠Y
B) ∠C = ∠Z
C) ∠C = ∠Z and $\overline{AC} = \overline{XZ}$
D) ∠C = ∠Z and ∠B = ∠Y

You should know these principles on angles and triangles for your exam:

The sum of all three angles in any triangle must be equal to 180 degrees.

An isosceles triangle has two equal sides and two equal angles.

An equilateral triangle has three equal sides and three equal angles.

Angles that have the same measurement in degrees are called congruent angles.

Equilateral triangles are also called congruent triangles.

Obtuse angles are more than 90 degrees, but less than 180 degrees.

Acute angles are less than 90 degrees.

Two angles are supplementary if they add up to 180 degrees. This means that when the two angles are placed together, they will form a straight line on one side.

Two angles are complementary (sometimes called adjacent angles) if they add up to 90 degrees. This means that the two angles will form a right angle.

The sides of a 30°–60°–90° triangle are in the ratio of 1:$\sqrt{3}$: 2.

The sides of a 45°–45°–90° triangle are in the ratio of 1: 1: $\sqrt{2}$.

36. The diagram below shows a figure made from a semicircle, a rectangle, and an equilateral triangle. The rectangle has a length of 18 inches and a width of 10 inches. What is the perimeter of the figure?

   A) 56 inches + 5π inches
   B) 56 inches + 10π inches
   C) 56 inches + 12.5π inches
   D) 56 inches + 25π inches

Tip: For questions on hybrid shapes or multi-sided figures, divide the figure into smaller shapes to solve. Here, the question clearly states that we have a semicircle, a rectangle, and an equilateral triangle. However, you may also see questions on hexagons or octagons on the exam. So, you should remember that a hexagon is made up of six equilateral triangles, while an octagon is made up of a central square, with four identical rectangles on each side of the central square and four identical triangles at the corners.

37. Nuclear waste is stored inside a spherical tank that is inscribed in a concrete cube, and the diameter of the sphere is 4 meters. Which one of the following must be false? (Use 3.14 for $π$.)
   A) The surface area of the cube is 96 square meters.
   B) The number for the surface area of the cube in square meters is larger than the number for the volume of the entire cube in cubic meters.
   C) The volume of the cube outside of the sphere is identical to the volume of the sphere.
   D) The volume of the cube outside of the sphere is approximately 30.5 cubic meters.

Tip: When a sphere is inscribed inside a cube, the diameter of the sphere is the same as the side length of the cube. The diameter of the sphere is 4 meters, so the side length of the cube is also 4 meters. Substitute this value into the formulas for cubes, and then check your calculations against the answer choices.

38. What is the slope of the line $\frac{1}{4}x - \frac{1}{5}y = 10$?
   A) −50
   B) $\frac{5}{4}$
   C) $\frac{1}{4}$
   D) $-\frac{1}{4}$

Tip: Isolate y on one side of the equation to put the equation into the slope-intercept form. The slope-intercept form is $y = mx + b$, where m is the slope, and b is the y-intercept.

39. Point (3, 4) is on a circle with a radius of 5 at angle θ. Find cos(θ) and sin(θ).

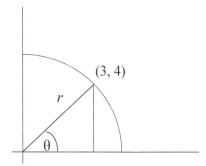

(3, 4)

r

θ

A) $\cos(\theta) = \frac{5}{3}$ and $\sin(\theta) = \frac{5}{4}$

B) $\cos(\theta) = \frac{3}{5}$ and $\sin(\theta) = \frac{4}{5}$

C) $\cos(\theta) = \frac{4}{5}$ and $\sin(\theta) = \frac{3}{5}$

D) $\cos(\theta) = \frac{5}{4}$ and $\sin(\theta) = \frac{5}{3}$

Tip: Refer to the trigonometric identifies on the formula sheet. You will also need to know the following: The sine function: $\sin(\theta) = \frac{y}{r}$, where r is the radius and y refers to coordinate y. The cosine function: $\cos(\theta) = \frac{x}{r}$, where r is the radius and x refers to the x-coordinate.

---

40. Evaluate for x: $\sin\left(\frac{\pi}{2}\right) = x + 2$
    A) 1
    B) 2
    C) –2
    D) –1

Be sure that you are well acquainted with the rules for sine and cosine that follow:

$\sin\left(\frac{\pi}{2}\right) = 1$ $\sin\left(\frac{\pi}{4}\right) = \frac{\sqrt{2}}{2}$ $\sin\left(\frac{\pi}{6}\right) = \frac{1}{6}$

$\cos\left(\frac{\pi}{2}\right) = 0$ $\cos\left(\frac{\pi}{4}\right) = \frac{\sqrt{2}}{2}$ $\cos\left(\frac{\pi}{6}\right) = \frac{\sqrt{3}}{2}$

Classic Learning Test Practice Math Exam 2

1. Point $(6,-1)$ is reflected across the y-axis. If point $(10, 3)$ is on the same reflected line, then which of the following represents an equation of that line?
    A) $-22 = x - 4y$
    B) $-2 = x - 4y$
    C) $\frac{1}{4} = x - y$
    D) $\frac{1}{4} = x + y$

2. Which of the answers below is equivalent to the expression $3a^3$ if $3a = \frac{2}{b}$

    A) $\frac{8}{b^3}$

    B) $\frac{9}{8b^3}$

    C) $\frac{8}{9b^3}$

    D) $\frac{4}{3b}$

3. Read the information below and answer the question that follows.

    - If door A is locked with the red key, then door B is locked with the blue key.
    - If door B is locked with the blue key, then door C is locked with the green key.
    - The key that locks door B also locks door D.

    If door A is locked with the red key, then which of the following must be true?
    A) Door C is locked with the blue key.
    B) Door C is locked with the red key.
    C) Door D is locked with the blue key.
    D) Door D is locked with the red key.

4. In the figure below, lines A and B are parallel. What is the measurement in degrees of angle t?

    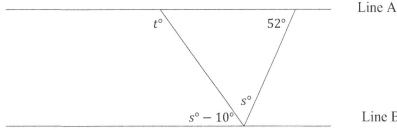

    A) 52
    B) 59
    C) 69
    D) 121

5. A local bingo hall has 10 extra-large bingo cards, 15 large bingo cards, 20 medium bingo cards, and 30 small bingo cards before any players arrive. Players are given a bingo card from the box at random upon arrival. The first player received an extra-large card and the second player received a small card. What is the percentage chance that the next player will receive a medium card?
   A) 24%
   B) 27.4%
   C) 28.8%
   D) 5.0%

6. A clothing store always chooses two styles from its various product lines to display by the cash register each day as the "deals of the day." It normally has 35 different product lines in stock. However, at the start of business one day, all of its socks, jeans, and t-shirts are out of stock. What is the chance that a denim jacket will be on display that day?
   A) 6.25%
   B) 5.71%
   C) 3.125%
   D) 2.85%

7. Which one of the points below is a solution to the following system of equations?
   $-3x - 1 = y$
   $x + 7 = y$
   A) $(5, -2)$
   B) $(-2, 5)$
   C) $(2, 5)$
   D) $(5, 2)$

8. In a particular section of a library, the ratio of non-fiction books to fiction books is $7:9$. The total number of fiction and non-fiction books in this section of the library is 128. If 10 fiction books and 14 non-fiction books are retired and removed from this section of the library, what is the new ratio of fiction books to the total of fiction and non-fiction books?
   A) $31:52$
   B) $21:31$
   C) $31:21$
   D) $9:13$

9. If $x + y = 5$ and $a + b = 4$, what is the value of $(3x + 3y)(5a + 5b)$?
   A) 9
   B) 35
   C) 200
   D) 300

10. Triangle ABC is similar to triangle XYZ and $\cos A = 0.98162718344$ and $\sin A = 0.19080899537$. Which of the following best approximates $\tan X$?
    A) 0.194
    B) 5.144
    C) 5.240
    D) Cannot be determined

11. How many numbers between 60 and 130 inclusive satisfy both of the following statements?
Statement 1: The first digit of the number is even.
Statement 2: The number is a prime number.
A) 0
B) 2
C) 3
D) 4

12. Martin is racing a car on a drag strip. The race may be represented by the following equation: $(d)m = -15m^2 + 30m + 45$, where m is equal to the time traveled in minutes and $(d)m$ is the distance traveled after m minutes in order to reach the finish line. How long does it take for Martin to pass the finish line?
A) 3 seconds
B) 30 seconds
C) 1 minute
D) 3 minutes

13. Consider the quadratic function $(x) = ax^2 + bx - c$, where $f(x) = y$. If m equals zero, how many real number solutions exist for the following equation: $ax^2 + bx - c = mx$?
A) 0
B) 1
C) 2
D) Cannot be determined.

14. Which of the following is an equation of a line that is perpendicular to the one that passes through (0, 3) and (10, –2)?
A) $y = {}^1/_2x + 3$

B) $y = 2x + 3$

C) $y = -x + 3$

D) $y = -{}^1/_2x + 3$

15. Angle A of triangle ABC measures 52° and angle C measures 38°. Based on these facts, which one of the following statements is false?
A) Side AB and side AC will have unequal measurements.
B) Triangle ABC is a right triangle.
C) The hypotenuse of triangle ABC is longer than either of the other two sides.
D) The area of the triangle can be determined using trigonometric identities.

16. If $\ominus$ is a special operation defined by $(x \ominus y) = (5x + 2y)$ and $(6 \ominus y) = 44$, then $y = ?$
A) 32
B) 36
C) 7
D) 17

17. If Q is an odd integer, then which of the following is also an odd integer?
A) 4Q
B) $Q^5 + 1$

C) $(2Q)^{-2}$
D) $Q^3 - 2$

18. The triangle in the illustration below is an equilateral triangle. What is the measurement in degrees of angle a?

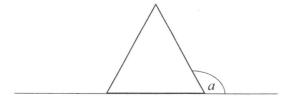

   A) 45°
   B) 60°
   C) 120°
   D) 180°

19. Which one of the answers below satisfies the following inequality? $7 - |2x - 5| < 4$
   A) $x = 1$
   B) $x > 4$ and $x < 1$
   C) $1 < x < 4$
   D) $x < 4$ or $x > 1$

20. Find the area in square inches of a regular hexagon in which the side length of one side is 8 inches.
   A) $16\sqrt{3}$
   B) $96\sqrt{3}$
   C) $192\sqrt{3}$
   D) Cannot be determined.

21. Find the equivalent to the following expression when $b^2 = a = c^3$:

$$\frac{10a^2b^4c^5}{5ab^2c^2}$$

   A) $2a^3$

   B) $2a^3b^6c^7$

   C) $5a^3b^6c^7$

   D) $5a^3$

22. Which one of the following right-angled triangles has the longest adjacent side?
    A) A right-angled triangle with an opposite side length of 6 inches and hypotenuse length of 9 inches.
    B) A right-angled triangle with an opposite side length of 8 inches and hypotenuse length of 12 inches.

    C) A right-angled triangle with an opposite side length of 13 inches and hypotenuse length of 16 inches.
    D) A right-angled triangle with an opposite side length of 5 inches and hypotenuse length of 10 inches.

23. The graph of y = f(x) is show below. Which of the following equations could define f(x)?

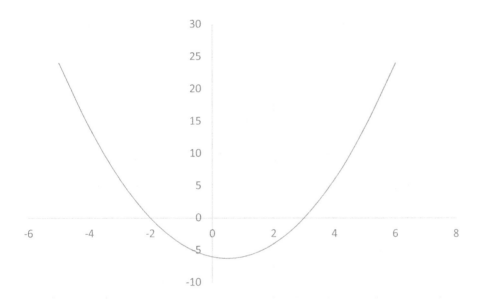

    A) $f(x) = (x - 3)(x + 2)$
    B) $f(x) = (x + 3)(x + 2)$
    C) $f(x) = (-2x - 3)(x + 2)$
    D) $f(x) = (-x - 3)(x + 2)$

24. The equation $(x + 3)^2 + y^2 = 64$ represents a circle in the xy-coordinate plane. Determine the area of the circle.
    A) 16π
    B) 32π
    C) 64π
    D) 128π

25. In the figure below, the length of XZ is 12 units, sin 30° = 0.5, cos 30° = 0.86603, and tan 30° = 0.57735. Approximately how many units long is XY?

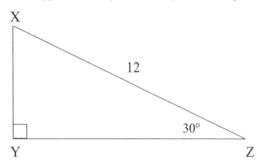

A) 5
B) 5.7735
C) 6
D) 8.6603

26. A property developer is constructing a penthouse apartment on the top floor of a circular tower. The floor of the tower in the penthouse is 15 meters across at its widest point. An arc on the penthouse wall corresponding to an angle of 120° will be covered with windows. No other windows will be placed in the penthouse. How long is the part of the wall that will be without windows?

A) 10π
B) 5π
C) $45\pi/2$
D) $20\pi/3$

27. A tennis club stores tennis balls in a wooden storage bin. The storage bin is a cube shape, with a side length of 2 feet 6 inches. Each tennis ball is a perfect sphere and has a diameter of 2.5 inches. At the end of training sessions each day, the tennis balls are placed into the storage cube, with the bottom completely covered with balls and additional layers of balls placed on top of this, until the cube is completely full. What is the maximum number of tennis balls that can be placed into the storage cube?

A) 36
B) 144
C) 1,728
D) 3,375

28. Find the solution to the system of inequalities:

$-2x - 8 < 30$
$x^3 + 12 < 76$

A) $-19 < x < 4$
B) $-19 > x > 4$
C) $-19 > x < 4$
D) $x > -19$

29. If $\sin \zeta = \frac{1}{\sqrt{2}}$, find the value of $\cot \zeta$.

A) $\pm\frac{1}{\sqrt{2}}$

B) $\pm\sqrt{2}$

C) 1

D) Cannot be determined.

30. Which line has the smallest slope?
    A) A line with an x-intercept of -4 and a y-intercept of 16.
    B) A line with an x-intercept of -3 that passes through (4, 14).
    C) A line with a y-intercept of 5 that passes through (9, 7).
    D) A line that passes through the points (0, -3) and (1, 11).

31. A company processes dairy products. Milk is stored in a spherical storage tank that is 72 inches across on the inside at its widest point. The tank is now 80% full of milk. Which one of the statements is false? (Use 3.14 for π)
    A) The surface area of the tank is approximately 16,278 square inches.
    B) The volume of the tank at full capacity is approximately 195,333 square inches.
    C) The diameter of the sphere is 36 inches.
    D) The volume of milk in the tank is approximately 165,267 square inches.

32. The ratio of the revolutions per minute of tire T to tire R is 5: 8. The speed of tire T is 150 revolutions per minute (RPM). If the RPM of a third tire, tire S, 25% faster than that of tire R, then what is the RPM of tire S?
    A) 300
    B) 180
    C) 117
    D) 70

33. Which of the following is not equivalent to $2\cos^2 \theta + \frac{1-\sin^2\theta}{\tan^2\theta}$

A) $2(1 - \sin^2\theta) + \frac{\cos^2\theta}{\tan^2\theta}$

B) $2(1 - \sin^2\theta) \dfrac{\cos^2\theta}{(\sin^2\theta \div \cos^2\theta)}$

C) $2\cos^2\theta + \dfrac{(1-\sin^2\theta)\cos^2\theta}{\sin^2\theta}$

D) $\sin^2\theta + 2$

34. Circle A has an area of approximately 113.04 inches. The diameter of Circle B is 20 inches. Circle C has an area of approximately 141.3 square inches more than Circle A. Rank the radii of these three circles from least to greatest. (Use 3.14 for π)
    A) Circle C, Circle A, Circle B
    B) Circle B, Circle A, Circle C
    C) Circle A, Circle C, Circle B
    D) Circle B, Circle C, Circle A

35. How many numbers between 500 and 599 inclusive satisfy both of the statements below?
    Statement 1: One digit of the number is 3, while the other digits are even.
    Statement 2: The sum of all three digits of the number is odd.
    A) 0
    B) 5
    C) 10
    D) 30

36. Find the period and amplitude of $y = \frac{5}{2}\cos\left(\frac{x}{4}\right)$.

    A) amplitude $= \frac{2}{5}$; period $= 2\pi$

    B) amplitude $= \frac{1}{4}$; period $= \frac{5}{2}\pi$

    C) amplitude $= \frac{5}{2}$; period $= 8\pi$

    D) amplitude $= \frac{5}{2}$; period $= \frac{1}{4}\pi$

37. A cylindrical container, which is 10 feet high and has a diameter of 7, is 55% full of saline solution. A pharmaceutical company wants to create a suspension of 3 liters of drug A for every 5 cubic feet of saline solution. If they use the saline solution that is currently in the tank, how many liters of drug A should they add?
    A) 122.5π
    B) 67.375π
    C) 40.425π
    D) 13.475π

38. Find the next term in the following sequence:

    $$\frac{1}{46}, \frac{1}{27}, \frac{1}{12}, 1 \ldots$$

    A) $1/6$

    B) $-1/6$

    C) $1/8$

    D) $1/3$

39. For the functions $f_2(x)$ listed below, x and y are integers greater than 1. If $f_1(x) = x^2$, which of the functions below has the greatest value for $f_1(f_2(x))$?
A) $f_2(x) = x/y$
B) $f_2(x) = y/x$
C) $f_2(x) = xy$
D) $f_2(x) = x - y$

40. Tom and Toni have just finished making 12 costumes for the drama club. They spent 40 hours working together to make the costumes, with Toni making costumes at a constant rate of one every 5 hours. Tom has just discovered that 4 more costumes are needed and that he will have to work alone to make them. How long will it take him to make these 4 extra costumes?
A) 8 hours
B) 10 hours
C) 40 hours
D) 48 hours

Classic Learning Test Practice Math Exam 3

1. A cafe sells both apples and oranges for lunch. They always have twice as many apples on stock as oranges. They have 24 apples for sale today. How many oranges do they have?
   A) 6
   B) 12
   C) 36
   D) 48

2. Which of the following is an equation of a line on the *xy*-coordinate plane that passes through the origin and is parallel to a line that passes through points $(0, 2)$ and $(-5, -1)$?
   A) $y = {}^3/_5x + 2$

   B) $y = {}^3/_5x + 0$

   C) $y = -{}^3/_5x + 2$

   D) $y = -{}^3/_5x + 0$

3. Fatima and Ashar are washing cars as part of a high school fund-raising event. Fatima can wash a car in 30 minutes, while Ashar can wash a car in 20 minutes. How long will it take them to wash five cars if they work together?
   A) 50 minutes
   B) 1 hour
   C) 1 hour and 15 minutes
   D) 2 hours and 5 minutes

4. Which of the following is equivalent to $2ab^2(3ab^3 + 2b)$?
   A) $6a^2b^5 + 4ab^3$
   B) $6a^2b^6 + 4ab^3$
   C) $6a^2b^5 + 4ab^2$
   D) $6a^2b^6 + 4ab^2$

5. The equation for the sum of the measurements of the inside angles of a polygon is as follows: $180(n - 2)° = S$, where *n* is the number of sides and *S* is the sum of the measurements. Calculate *S* for a polygon with twenty sides.
   A) 3,240°
   B) 3,420°
   C) 3,568°
   D) 3,600°

6. How many integers between 1 and 200 inclusive are the product of 14 and another integer?
   A) 7
   B) 9
   C) 14
   D) 20

7. A deck of cards contains 13 hearts, 13 diamonds, 13 clubs, and 13 spades. Cards are selected from the deck at random. Once selected, the cards are discarded and are not placed back into the deck. Two spades, one heart, and a club are drawn from the deck. What is the probability that the next card drawn from the deck will be a heart?

A) 7.69%

B) 8.33%

C) 24%

D) 25%

8. The figure below shows a right triangular prism. Side AB measures 3 units, side AC measures 4 units, and side BD measures 7 units. What amount below best approximates the total surface area of this triangular prism in square units?

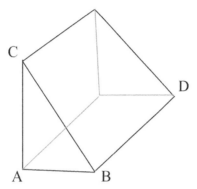

A) 64
B) 77
C) 90
D) 96

9. If $x = -1$. What does $x + x^2 + x^3 + \ldots x^{12}$ equal?
A) -1
B) 0
C) 1
D) $i + 1$

10. Find the equivalent: $(a^3 b)^4$
A) $a^7 b^5$
B) $a^{12} b^4$
C) $a^3 b^4$
D) $a^{-1} b^{-4}$

11. A footstool is cube-shaped, and each side of the footstool is divided into 9 equal-sized squares. Each square will be made up of either beige or brown fabric, and there need to be at least three squares of each color on every side of the cube. What is the maximum number of brown-colored fabric pieces that the footstool could have in total?
    A) 18
    B) 24
    C) 36
    D) 54

12. If $x + y = 5$ and $a + b = 4$, what is the value of $(4x + 4y)(6a + 6b)$?
    A) 20
    B) 24
    C) 44
    D) 480

13. The distance around the outside of a basketball hoop measures 18π inches. What is the measurement in inches across the widest point of the basketball hoop?
    A) 81
    B) 36
    C) 18
    D) 9

14. Find the next term in the following geometric sequence:

$$\frac{3}{5}, 1, ?, \frac{25}{9}$$

    A) $\frac{1}{5}$

    B) $\frac{9}{25}$

    C) $\frac{5}{3}$

    D) $\frac{3}{5}$

15. In the right triangle below, the length of AC is 10 units and the length of BC is 8 units. What is the tangent of $\angle A$?

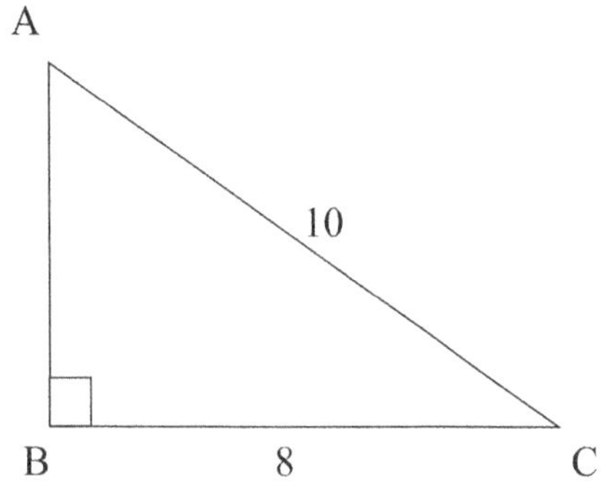

A) 3/4
B) 4/3
C) 6
D) 3/5

16. Special operation Φ is defined as follows: $a \Phi b = 3^a - 4^b$. What is the value when of this special operation when $a = -2$ and $b = 2$?

   A) $-\dfrac{129}{9}$

   B) $-\dfrac{159}{16}$

   C) $-\dfrac{145}{9}$

   D) $-\dfrac{143}{9}$

17. How many integers between 15 and 130 inclusive satisfy both of the conditions given below?
   Condition 1: The integer is even.
   Condition 2: The integer is divisible by 13 without a remainder.
   A) 5
   B) 6
   C) 9
   D) 10

18. Which of the following statements about parallelograms is true?
   A) A parallelogram has no right angles.
   B) A parallelogram has opposite angles which are congruent.
   C) The opposite sides of a parallelogram are unequal in measure.
   D) A rectangle is not a parallelogram.

19. The illustration below shows an isosceles triangle. The entire triangle has a base of 9 and a height of 18.

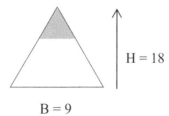

B = 9

The shaded portion at the top of the triangle has a height of 6. What fraction expresses the area of the shaded portion to the area of the entire triangle?

   A) $^1/_9$

   B) $^1/_2$

   C) $^1/_3$

   D) $^1/_{18}$

20. Two cars are traveling on the same route. Car C is traveling at a speed of 50 miles per hour and begins the journey at 10:00 AM. Car D begins the journey at 10:30 AM at a speed of 60 miles per hour. At how many miles into the journey will car D meet car C?
A) 120
B) 125
C) 150
D) 180

21. Find the value of x for the system of equations:
$x + y - z = -1$
$x + 3y = 13$
$x + 3y + 2z = 17$
A) −5
B) −2
C) 5
D) 6

22. The triangle in the xy-plane below will be rotated 180° counterclockwise about the origin and then reflected across the x-axis to produce a new triangle. The coordinates of vertex A of the original triangle are (4, 0), and vertex A' of the new triangle will correspond to vertex A of the original triangle. Which one of the following could be the coordinates of vertex A' of the new triangle?

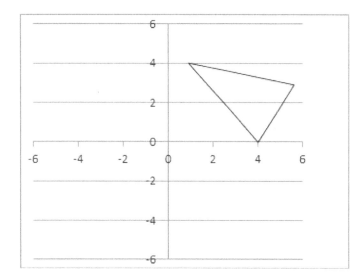

A) (−4, 0)
B) (0, −4)
C) (4, 0)
D) (0, 4)

23. AB and CD are parallel and lengths are provided in units. What is the area of trapezoid ABCD in square units? (The figure is not drawn to scale.)

A) 24
B) 30
C) 34
D) 36

24. The two figures below are similar. The side lengths of each figure are provided in inches. Calculate the perimeter in inches of figure KLMN. (The figures are not drawn to scale.)

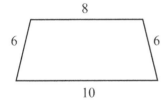
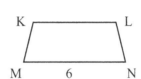

A) 16
B) 18
C) 24
D) 30

25. Which of the equations provided below is sufficient to illustrate that the following statement is false?

If $x \times y$ can be divided by 6, then x is divisible by 6 or y is divisible by 6.

A) $4 \times 5 = 20$
B) $3 \times 4 = 12$
C) $6 \times 3 = 18$
D) $5 \times 6 = 30$

26. Which of the following number lines represents seven values in which the range of the values exceeds the median, and the median of the values exceeds the mean?

A)

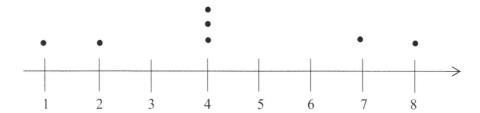

B)

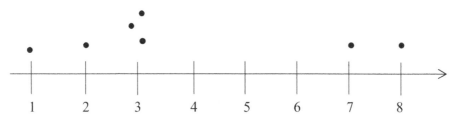

C)

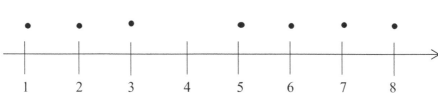

D)

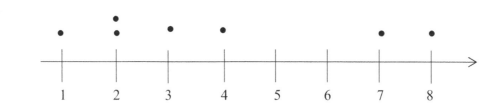

27. How many integers between 200 and 699 inclusive satisfy both conditions below:
Condition 1: The number is divisible by 8
Condition 2: The number is not divisible by 9.
A) 54
B) 56
C) 57
D) 63

28. A sporting goods company is going to ship a javelin to an athlete training for the javelin throw in the Olympics. The company sending the javelin, which is shaped like a spear, places the item inside a box so that the smallest size box can be used. The box measures 3 feet by 3 feet by 8 feet. Approximately how long is the javelin?
A) 7.5 feet
B) 8 feet
C) 8.5 feet
D) 9 feet

29. Which transformation of the function $y = \sin \theta$ yields a function with an amplitude of 2 and a period of $\frac{\pi}{2}$?

A) $y = 2\sin\theta + 4$

B) $y = 2\sin 4\theta$

C) $y = 4 \sin \frac{\theta}{\pi}$

D) $y = 2 \sin\theta$

30. A sporting goods store displays golf balls inside a larger, hollow golf ball display case. The display case is a perfect sphere and is 1,280 millimeters (mm) in diameter. The golf galls are suspended in a single row across three pieces of invisible fishing line inside the case, and the diameters of the golf balls line up exactly with the diameter of the case. Each golf ball is 40 mm in diameter. What is the approximate volume of the space inside the display case excluding the space taken up by the balls when all of the balls are lined up in it?

A) $349,098,667\pi$ mm

B) $349,514,667\pi$ mm

C) $349,184,000\pi$ mm

D) $349,525,333\pi$ mm

31. Find the values of x and y at the point or points of intersection of the following parabolas:
$y = -x^2 + 6x - 6.5$ and $y = x^2 - 2$

A) $(0.25, 1.5)$

B) $(1.5 , 0.25)$

C) $(1.5 , 0.25)$ and $(-1.5 , -0.25)$

D) $(0.25, 1.5)$ and $(-0.25, -1.5)$

32. If $\cos A = 0.30902$ and $\sin A = 0.95106$, then $\tan A = ?$

A) 3.07767

B) 0.307767

C) 0.32492

D) 0.04894

33. A motorcycle traveled 38.4 miles in $^4/_5$ of an hour. What was the speed of the motorcycle in miles per hour?

A) 9.6

B) 30.72

C) 48

D) 52

34. The length of arc PQ is 4π units. If the two rays form a 32° angle, then which of the following statements is false? (Note that the drawing is not to scale and you should use 3.14 for π.)

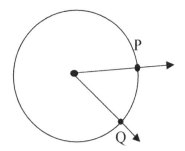

    A) The diameter of the circle is approximately 45 units.
    B) The circumference of the circle is approximately 141.3 units.
    C) The area of the circle is approximately 1,950 units.
    D) The radius of the circle is approximately 22.5 units.

35. If x represents a real number, what is the greatest possible value of $8 \times \sin 2x$?
    A) 8
    B) 4
    C) 2
    D) 1/2

36. Which one of the integers below satisfies the following condition?
    The sum of the digits of the integer is 2 more than the number of its distinct factors.
    A) 5
    B) 15
    C) 32
    D) 64

37. Find the area in square inches of an octagon that has one side measuring $5\sqrt{2}$ inches.
    A) $100\sqrt{2} + 100$
    B) $125\sqrt{2} + 50$
    C) $155\sqrt{2} + 50$
    D) Cannot be determined

38. 2 inches on a scale drawing represents F feet. Which of the following equations represents $F + 1$ feet on the drawing?
    A) $\frac{2(F+1)}{F}$

    B) $\frac{(F+1)}{F}$

    C) $\frac{2}{F+1}$

    D) $\frac{2F}{F+1}$

39. The radius (R) of circle A is 5 centimeters. The radius of circle B is 3 centimeters. Which of the following statements is true?

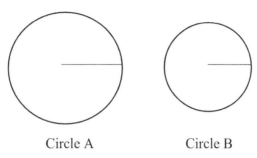

Circle A   Circle B

A) The difference between the areas of the circles is 2π.
B) The difference between the areas of the circles is 9π.
C) The difference between the circumferences of the circles is 2π.
D) The difference between the circumferences of the circles is 4π.

40. Point R on the circle is rotated about the origin of the *xy*-coordinate plane until it rests on point S, which lies on the *y*-axis. Which one of the following statements best describes this transformation?

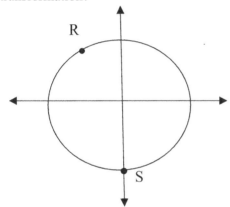

A) $\frac{5\pi}{6}$ radians clockwise

B) $\frac{\pi}{2}$ radians clockwise

C) $\frac{5\pi}{6}$ radians counterclockwise

D) $\frac{5\pi}{4}$ radians counterclockwise

Classic Learning Test Practice Math Exam 4

1. What is the value of $f_1(2)$ where $f_1(x) = 49^{1/x}$?
   A) $\sqrt{7}$
   B) $49/2$
   C) $49/\sqrt{x}$
   D) 7

2. What is the range of $y \leq -5x^4 - 8$?
   A) $y \geq -8$
   B) $y \leq -8$
   C) $y \leq 8$
   D) $y \geq 8$

3. Perform the operation and simplify:

   $$\frac{3a^2}{4} \times \frac{2}{a^3} = ?$$

   A) $\dfrac{3}{2a}$

   B) $\dfrac{5a^2}{4a^3}$

   C) $\dfrac{8}{3a^5}$

   D) $\dfrac{8}{3a^6}$

4. Complete the square and then simplify if possible: $x^2 - 8x + 1 = 0$
   A) $x = \pm\sqrt{15} + 8$
   B) $x = \pm\sqrt{15} - 4$
   C) $x = \pm\sqrt{15} + 4$
   D) $x = \pm\sqrt{15} + 16$

5. Use the information below to answer the question that follows.

   - Classes in the morning last for 45 minutes, but classes in the afternoon last for 50 minutes.
   - Lunch begins promptly at 12:30 pm and finishes promptly at 1:00 pm.
   - There are 3 classes after lunch and 4 classes before lunch.
   - There are no breaks between classes or between classes and lunch.

   Which one of the following statements could be true?
   A) Classes begin at 9:30am.
   B) Classes begin at 10:00am.

C) The second class after lunch begins at 2:00pm.
D) The second class after lunch begins at 2:50pm.

6. Solve for x: $x^2 - 11x < -24$
   A) $3 < x > 8$
   B) $3 < x < 8$
   C) $3 > x > 8$
   D) $3 > x < 8$

7. Which of the following is a function where $y = f(x)$?
   A)

   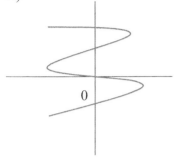

   B)

   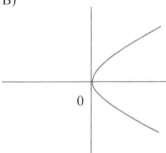

   C)

   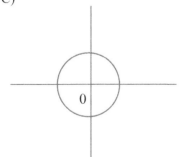

D)

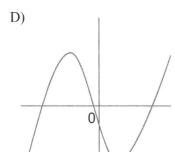

8. The median and mean of 9 numbers are 8 and 9 respectively. The 9 numbers are positive integers greater than zero. If each of the 9 numbers is increased by 2, which of the following must be true of the increased numbers?
A) The mean will be greater than before, but the median will remain the same.
B) The median will be greater than before, but the mean will remain the same.
C) Both the median and mean will be greater than before.
D) The median and mean will be the same as before, but the range will increase.

9. A magician pulls colored scarves out of a hat at random. The hat contains 5 red scarves and 6 blue scarves. The other scarves in the hat are green. If a scarf is pulled out of the hat at random, the probability that the scarf is red is $^1/_3$. How many green scarves are in the hat?
A) 3
B) 4
C) 5
D) 6

10. Darnella wants to put wooden trim around the floor of her family room. Each piece of trim is 18 inches in length. The room is rectangular and is 12 feet long and 10 feet wide. The trim will be put around all of the wall, apart from the area for the door and its trim, which is 35 inches wide. She prefers to use as many whole pieces of trim as possible in order to minimize the number of joints between the pieces. How many pieces of trim does Darnella need for this job?
A) 20
B) 26
C) 27
D) 28

11. The kinetic energy (KE) associated with an object is calculated as $KE = \frac{1}{2}mv^2$, where m is the mass of an object and v is the velocity. An apple falls from an apple tree, where m_1 is the mass of the apple, and v_1 is the velocity. A pear with double the mass of and 25% more velocity than the apple falls from a pear tree. What is the ratio of the kinetic energy of the apple to the kinetic energy of the pear?

A) $\frac{1}{2}$

B) 2

C) $\frac{8}{25}$

D) $\frac{25}{8}$

12. The values in the table below represent a line on the *xy*-graph that forms the diameter of a circle with a radius of 3 which is centered around the origin of the same graph. What is the approximate circumference of the circle?

x	y
–4	4
–3	3
–2	2
–1	1
0	0
1	–1
2	–2
3	–3
4	–4

A) 3π

B) 6

C) 6π

D) 9

13. If y^3 is a negative even integer, and $x + y$ is a negative integer, then xy would be:
   A) A positive odd integer
   B) A negative odd integer
   C) A positive or negative even integer
   D) A positive or negative odd integer

14. In triangle XYZ, ∠X is a right angle. Side XY is opposite to ∠Z and side XZ is adjacent to ∠Z. Side YZ forms the hypotenuse. Side XY is 9 units long, side XZ is 12 units long, and side YZ is 15 units long. Which fraction below represents sin Z?
   A) $^{15}/_9$
   B) $^{9}/_{15}$
   C) $^{12}/_{15}$
   D) $^{9}/_{12}$

15. How many real number solutions exist for the following equation? $y = ^1/_{\sqrt{-x}}$

   A) 0
   B) 1
   C) 2
   D) An infinite number of solutions exist.

16. Find all of the points on the graph $x^2 + y^2 = 9$ where the tangent lines satisfy both of the following statements:

    Statement 1 – The tangent lines are horizontal or vertical.

    Statements – The points of tangency lie on the axes between the first and second quadrants or the second and third quadrants.

    A) $(0, -3)$ and $(3, 0)$
    B) $(0, 3)$ and $(3, 0)$
    C) $(0, 3)$ and $(-3, 0)$
    D) $(0, -3)$ and $(-3, 0)$

17. Use the diagram below to answer the question that follows.

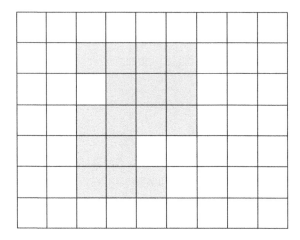

    Each square in the diagram above is four feet wide and four feet long. The gray area of the diagram represents the layout of a water reservoir. What is the perimeter in feet of the reservoir?
    A) 22 feet
    B) 87 feet
    C) 88 feet
    D) 100 feet

18. Consider two concentric circles with radii of $R_1 = 1$ and $R_2 = 2.4$ as shown in the illustration below. Line L forms the diameter of the circles. What is the area of the lined part of the illustration?

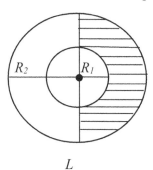

    L

    A) 0.7π
    B) 1.4π

C) 2π

D) 2.38π

19. What equation represents the slope-intercept formula for the following data?

Through (4, 5); $m = -\frac{3}{5}$

A) $y = -\frac{3}{5}x + 5$

B) $y = -\frac{12}{5}x - 5$

C) $y = -\frac{3}{5}x - \frac{37}{5}$

D) $y = -\frac{3}{5}x + \frac{37}{5}$

20. Solve for x and y:

$6x + 3y + z = 26$

$10x + 6y + 3z = 30$

$x \div 6 = z$

A) $x = 2$, $y = 2$, and $z = -2$

B) $x = -12$, $y = 16$, and $z = 1$

C) $x = 2$, $y = 4$, and $z = 1$

D) $x = 12$, $y = -16$, and $z = 2$

21. If the radius of a circle is 3 and the radians of the subtended angle measure $^\pi/_3$, what is the length of the arc subtending the central angle?

A) $^\pi/_3$

B) $^\pi/_9$

C) π

D) 3π

22. Examine the illustration below and answer the question that follows.

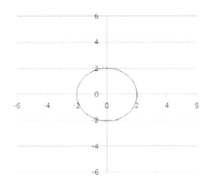

Which of the following points could be the intersection of the circle and the line x = −2?

A) (0,−2)

B) (2, 0)

C) (0, 2)

D) (−2, 0)

23. The base (B) of the cylinder in the illustration shown below is at a right angle to its sides. The radius (R) of the base of cylinder measures 5 centimeters. A circular plane that is perpendicular to the base is placed inside the cylinder. Which of the following could be true about this perpendicular circular plane?

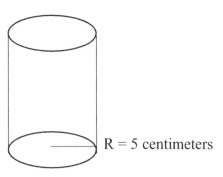

R = 5 centimeters

A) Its radius is equal to R.
B) Its radius is greater than 5.
C) Its radius is greater than 10.
D) It will be double the size of B.

24. In the figure below, the circle centered at B is internally tangent to the circle centered at A. The length of line segment AB, which represents the radius of circle A, is 3 units and the center of the smaller circle passes through the center of the larger circle. If the area of the smaller circle is removed from the larger circle, what is the remaining area of the larger circle? (The drawing not to scale.)

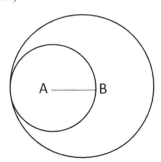

A) 3π
B) 6π
C) 9π
D) 27π

25. If the pattern continues, what is the next item in the following list? $\dfrac{1}{4}, \dfrac{5}{8}, \dfrac{9}{12}, \dfrac{13}{16}$

A) $\dfrac{14}{20}$

B) $\dfrac{17}{20}$

C) $\dfrac{18}{19}$

D) $\dfrac{21}{19}$

26. Use the information provided in the box below to answer the question that follows.

> - The gas station is 10 miles away from the grocery store.
> - The grocery store is 6 miles away from the hotel.

Based on the information in the box, what conclusions can be made?
A) The gas station is no more than 6 miles away from the hotel.
B) The gas station is no more than 10 miles away from the hotel.
C) The gas station is exactly 6 miles away from the hotel.
D) The gas station is no more than 16 miles away from the hotel.

27. The perimeter of a rectangle is 48 meters. If the length were doubled and the width were increased by 5 meters, the perimeter would be 92 meters. What are the length and width of the original rectangle?
A) width = 7, length = 17
B) width = 17, length = 7
C) width = 34, length = 14
D) width = 24, length = 46

28. ∠A measures 42° and cos A = sin B. What is the sum of ∠A + ∠B?
A) 42°
B) 21°
C) 90°
D) 48°

29. 5 more than 4 times the number x is equal to the number y minus the number z.
Which statement below represents this equation?
A) $5x + 4 = y + z$
B) $4x + 5 = y - z$
C) $4(x + 5) = y - z$
D) $4(y + 5) = x - z$

30. AB is 6 inches long and AC is 9 inches long. What is the area of triangle ABC?

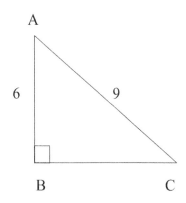

A) 27
B) $3\sqrt{5}$
C) $\left(3\sqrt{5} \times 3\right)$
D) $\left(3\sqrt{5} \times 6\right) \div 2$

31. The parabola represented by the equation $y = x^2$ stretched vertically by a factor of 3. Then it is moved up by 2 units and right by 4 units. Which of the following represents the equation of the new line.
A) $y - 2 = 3(x - 4)^2$
B) $y + 2 = 3x^2 + 4$
C) $y + 2 = 3(x + 4)^2$
D) $3(y + 2) = x^2 + 4$

32. Which of the following equations could define $f(x)$?

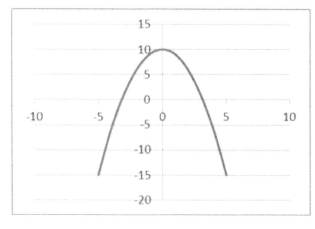

A) $f(x) = x + 10$
B) $f(x) = x^2 - 10$
C) $f(x) = x^2 + 10$
D) $f(x) = -(x^2) + 10$

33. The illustration below shows a pentagon. The shaded part at the top of the pentagon has a height of 6 inches. (The drawing is not to scale.)

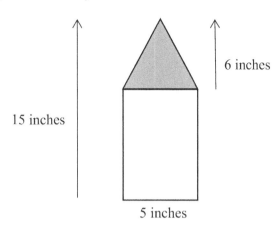

The height of the entire pentagon is 15 inches, and the base of the pentagon is 5 inches. What fraction expresses the area of the shaded part to the area of the entire pentagon? State your answer as a simplified fraction in the spaces provided.
A) 1/4
B) 1/3
C) 3/5
D) 1/5

34. Indicate which of the following statements are true for all positive numbers x, y and z.

Statement I: $x \times (y + z) = (y + z) \times x$

Statement II: $x - (y + z) = x - y + z$

Statement III: $x \times (y + z) = (x \times y) + z$

Statement IV: $x + (y - z) = (x + y) - z$

A) I and II
B) I and III
C) I and IV
D) II and IV

35. Consider rectangular figure WXYZ below:

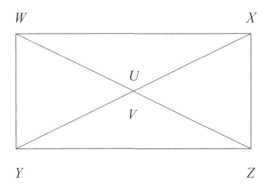

Which of the following must be true?
A) ∠YWX = ∠YWU
B) ∠YUW = ∠WUX
C) $\overline{WY} = \overline{UY}$
D) ∠WUX = ∠YVZ

36. In the figure below, the length of AC is 14 units, sin 55° = 0.8192, cos 55° = 0.5736, and tan 55° = 1.4281. Approximately how many units long is BC?

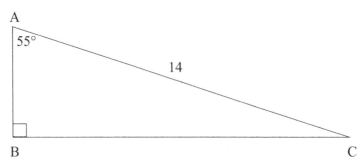

A) 0.8192
B) 19.9934
C) 8.0304
D) 11.469

37. cos *A* = 0.6156614 and sin *A* = 0.7880107, then tan *A* = ?
A) 1.279
B) 0.782
C) 1.269
D) 1.620

38. A kite is formed of two identical isosceles triangles that are joined together at their bases in the center of the kite. Each isosceles triangle has a base of 2 feet and a height of 3 feet. What is the perimeter measurement of the kite?
A) 6
B) 12
C) $2\sqrt{10}$
D) $4\sqrt{10}$

39. Which of the following could be an equation of the graph below?

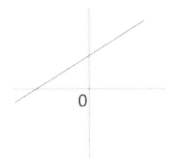

A) $y = x^2 + 3$
B) $y = x + 5$
C) $y = -x + 7$
D) $y = |x| - 5$

40. The rectangular cuboid in the illustration below has a length of 16 centimeters (cm), a width of 14 cm, and a volume of 2,016 cubic cm. If the length, width, and height are each increased by 20%, what is the volume of the enlarged cuboid in cubic centimeters?

16 cm

14 cm

A) 2903.04
B) 2419.20
C) 3483.648
D) 2036.00

CLT Practice Math Exam 5 – Algebra, Geometry, and Trigonometry Review

Manipulating Roots

1. Which of the answers below is equal to the following radical expression? $\sqrt{50}$
   A) $1 \div 50$
   B) $2\sqrt{25}$
   C) $2\sqrt{5}$
   D) $5\sqrt{2}$

   > Step 1: Factor the number inside the square root sign. Step 2: Look to see if any of the factors are perfect squares. In this case, the only factor that is a perfect square is 25. Step 3: Find the square root of 25 then simplify.

2. $\sqrt{36} + 4\sqrt{72} - 2\sqrt{144} = ?$
   A) $2\sqrt{36}$
   B) $2\sqrt{252}$
   C) $18 + 24\sqrt{2}$
   D) $-18 + 24\sqrt{2}$

   > Step 1: Find the common factors that are perfect squares. Step 2: Factor the amounts inside each of the radical signs and simplify.

3. $\sqrt{7} \times \sqrt{11} = ?$
   A) $\sqrt{77}$
   B) $\sqrt{18}$
   C) $7\sqrt{11}$
   D) $11\sqrt{7}$

   > Step 1: Multiply the numbers inside the radical signs. Step 2: Put this product inside a radical symbol for your answer.

4. Express as a rational number: $\sqrt[3]{\frac{216}{27}}$
   A) 3
   B) 2
   C) $\frac{7}{3}$
   D) $\sqrt[3]{2}$

   > Step 1: Find the cube roots of the numerator and denominator to eliminate the radical. The cube root is a number that equals the required product when multiplied by itself two times. Step 2: Simplify further if possible.

Manipulating Exponents

5. $7^5 \times 7^3 = ?$

    A) 7^8

    B) 7^{15}

    C) 14^8

    D) 49^8

> If the base number or variable is the same, you need to add the exponents when multiplying, but keep the base number or variable the same as before.

6. $(xy)^6 \div (xy)^3 = ?$

    A) $(xy)^{18}$

    B) $(xy)^3$

    C) $x^2 y^3$

    D) $(xy)^2$

> If the base or variable number is the same, you need to subtract the exponents when dividing, but keep the base number or variable the same as before.

7. $x^{\frac{5}{7}} = ?$

    A) $\frac{5x}{7}$

    B) $\left(\sqrt[5]{x}\right)^7$

    C) $\left(7\sqrt{x}\right)^5$

    D) $\left(\sqrt[7]{x}\right)^5$

> Step 1: Put the base number or variable inside the radical sign. Step 2: The denominator of the exponent is the nth root of the radical. Step 3: The numerator is the new exponent.

8. $x^{-5} = ?$

    A) $\frac{1}{x^{-5}}$

    B) $\frac{1}{x^5}$

C) −5x

D) $\frac{1}{5x}$

Step 1: Set up a fraction, where 1 is the numerator. Step 2: Put the term with the exponent in the denominator, but remove the negative sign on the exponent.

9. $62^0 = ?$

    A) −62

    B) 0

    C) 1

    D) 62

Any non-zero number raised to the power of zero is equal to 1.

Simplifying Rational Algebraic Expressions

10. $\dfrac{b + \frac{2}{7}}{\frac{1}{b}} = ?$

    A) $b^2 + \frac{7}{2}$

    B) $2b + \frac{7}{2}$

    C) $b^2 + \frac{2b}{7}$

    D) $\dfrac{b}{b + \frac{2}{7}}$

Step 1: When the expression has fractions in both the numerator and denominator, treat the line in the main fraction as the division symbol. Step 2: Invert the fraction that was in the denominator and multiply.

11. $\dfrac{x^2}{x^2 + 2x} + \dfrac{8}{x} = ?$

    A) $\dfrac{x + 8x + 16}{x^2 + 2x}$

    B) $\dfrac{x^2 + 8}{x^2 + 3x}$

C) $\dfrac{8x^2 + 16x}{x^3}$

D) $\dfrac{x^2 + 8x + 16}{x^2 + 2x}$

Step 1: Find the lowest common denominator. Since x is common to both denominators, we can convert the denominator of the second fraction to the LCD by multiplying the numerator and denominator of the second fraction by $(x + 2)$. Step 2: When you have both fractions in the LCD, add the numerators to solve.

Factoring Polynomials

12. Perform the operation and simplify: $\dfrac{2a^3}{7} \times \dfrac{3}{a^2} = ?$

A) $\dfrac{6a}{7}$

B) $\dfrac{5a^3}{7a^2}$

C) $\dfrac{2a^6}{21}$

D) $\dfrac{21}{2a^6}$

Step 1: Multiply the numerator of the first fraction by the numerator of the second fraction to get the new numerator. Step 2: Then multiply the denominators. Step 3: Factor out a^2 to simplify.

13. $\dfrac{8x + 8}{x^4} \div \dfrac{5x + 5}{x^2} = ?$

A) $\dfrac{5x^2}{8}$

B) $\dfrac{8}{5x^2}$

C) $\dfrac{3x+3}{x^2}$

D) $\dfrac{x^2 + 8x + 8}{x^4 + 5x + 5}$

Step 1: Invert and multiply by the second fraction. Step 2: Cancel out $(x + 1)$. Step 3: Cancel out x^2.

49

Expanding Polynomials

14. Expand the following equation: $(x + 4y)^2$

    A) $2(x + 8y)$

    B) $2x + 8y$

    C) $x^2 + 8xy^2 + 16y^2$

    D) $x^2 + 8xy + 16y^2$

> When expanding polynomials, you should use the FOIL method: First – Outside – Inside – Last. We can demonstrate the FOIL method on an example equation as follows:
> $(a + b)(c + d) = (a \times c) + (a \times d) + (b \times c) + (b \times d) = ac + ad + bc + bd$

Series and Sequences

15. What is the next number in the following sequence? 1, 1/6, 1/11, 1/16, 1/21, . . .

    A)   1/25

    B)   1/26

    C)   1/31

    D)   1/36

> Try to find the pattern between the numbers to solve. In this question, each subsequent term is found by adding. For a geometric sequence, each subsequent term is found by multiplying by a constant.

Quadratic Equations

16. Simplify: $(x - y)(x + y)$

    A) $x^2 - 2xy - y^2$

    B) $x^2 + 2xy - y^2$

    C) $x^2 + y^2$

    D) $x^2 - y^2$

> Use the FOIL method on quadratic equations like this one when the instructions tell you to simplify.

Linear Inequalities

17. $50 - \frac{3x}{5} \geq 41$, then $x \leq$?

    A)   15

    B)   25

    C)   41

    D)   50

> Step 1: Isolate the whole numbers to one side of the inequality. Step 2: Get rid of the fraction by multiplying each side by 5. Step 3: Divide to simplify further. Step 4: Isolate the variable to solve.

18. The cost of one wizfit is equal to y. If $x - 2 > 5$ and $y = x - 2$, then the cost of 2 wizfits is greater than which one of the following?

A) $x - 2$

B) $x - 5$

C) $y + 5$

D) 10

> Look to see if the inequality and the equation have any variables or terms in common. In this problem, both the inequality and the equation contain $x - 2$. The cost of one wizfit is represented by y, and y is equal to $x - 2$. So, we can substitute values from the equation into the inequality.

Quadratic Inequalities

19. Solve for x: $x^2 - 9 < 0$

A) $x < -3$ and $x > 3$

B) $x > -3$ and $x < 3$

C) $x < -3$ and $x < 3$

D) $x > -3$ and $x > 3$

> For quadratic inequality problems like this one, you need to factor the inequality first. We know that the factors of -9 are: -1×9; -3×3; 1×-9. We do not have a term with only the x variable, so we need factors that add up to zero. $-3 + 3 = 0$. So, try to solve the problem based on these facts. Be sure to check your work when you have found a solution.

Systems of Equations

20. What ordered pair is a solution to the following system of equations?

$x + y = 7$

$xy = 12$

A) $(2, 6)$

B) $(6, 2)$

C) $(4, 2)$

D) $(3, 4)$

> Step 1: Look at the multiplication equation and find the factors of 12. Step 2: Add the factors in each set together to see if they equal 7 to solve the addition in the first equation.

21. Solve by elimination: $3x + 3y = 15$ and $x + 2y = 8$

A) $x = -18$ and $y = 13$

B) $x = -2$ and $y = 3$

C) $x = 2$ and $y = 3$

D) $x = 3$ and $y = 2$

Step 1: Look at the x term of the first equation, which is $3x$. In order to eliminate the x variable, we need to multiply the second equation by 3. Step 2: Subtract this result from the first equation to solve.

Special Operations

22. If ζ is defined as $x \zeta y = \dfrac{x^4}{y^2} - 6$, then which of the following answers is equal to $2 \zeta 4$?

We have the special operation defined as $x \zeta y = \dfrac{x^4}{y^2} - 3$. First, substitute 2 for x and 4 for y in the fraction. Then perform the operations on the right side of the equation to solve.

A) −59

B) 59

C) 5

D) −5

Plane and Coordinate Geometry

23. The triangle in the illustration below is an isosceles triangle. What is the measurement of ∠B?

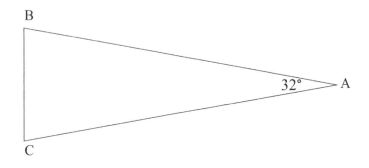

A) 32°

B) 45°

C) 74°

D) 148°

Step 1: Deduct the measurement of angle A from 180° to find out the total degrees of the two other angles. Step 2: Since we have an isosceles triangle, the other two angles are equal in measure.

24. The central angle in the circle below is 90° and is subtended by an arc which is 8π centimeters in length. How many centimeters long is the radius of this circle?

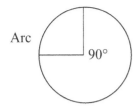

Arc

90°

A) 32
B) 16
C) 8π
D) 8

When working with arcs, you can calculate the radius or diameter of a circle if you have the measurement of a central angle and the length of the arc subtending the central angle. You will also need the formula for circumference: Circumference = $\pi \times$ radius $\times$ 2. You can think of arc length as part of the circumference.

25. A field is 100 yards long and 32 yards wide. What is the area of the field in square yards?
   A) 160
   B) 320
   C) 1600
   D) 3200

Area of a square or rectangle: length × width
Area of a circle: $\pi \times r^2$ (radius squared)
Area of a triangle: (base × height) ÷ 2

26. If a circle has a diameter of 6, what is the circumference of the circle?
   A) 6π
   B) 12π
   C) 24π
   D) 36π

Diameter = radius × 2
Remember that the formula for the circumference of a circle is $\pi \times$ diameter.

27. If a circle with center $(-5, 5)$ is tangent to the x axis in the standard (x, y) coordinate plane, what is the diameter of the circle?
   A) -5
   B) -10
   C) 5
   D) 10

Diameter is the measurement across the entire width of a circle. Diameter is always double the radius. If the center of a circle (x, y) is tangent to the x axis, then both of the following conditions are true: [1] The point of tangency is equal to $(x, 0)$ and [2] The distance between (x, y) and $(x, 0)$ is equal to the radius.

28. XY is 4 inches long and XZ is 5 inches long. What is the area of triangle XYZ? (The drawing is not to scale.)

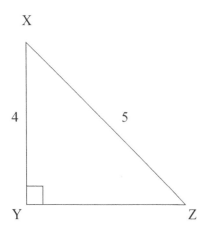

A) 3
B) 5
C) 6
D) 10

Step 1: Use the Pythagorean theorem to find the length of line segment XZ.
Hypotenuse length $C = \sqrt{A^2 + B^2}$
Step 2: Calculate the area of the triangle: (base × height) ÷ 2

29. In the figure below, ∠Y is a right angle and ∠X = 60°. If line segment YZ is 5 units long, then how long is line segment XY? (The drawing is not to scale.)

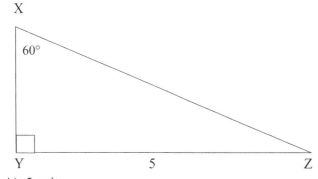

A) 5 units
B) 6 units

C) 15 units

D) $\frac{5}{\sqrt{3}}$ units

Triangle XYZ is a 30°–60°–90° triangle.

Using the Pythagorean theorem, its sides are therefore in the ratio of 1: $\sqrt{3}$: 2.

---

30. What is the perimeter of a rectangle that has a length of 17 and a width of 4?

    A) 21

    B) 34

    C) 42

    D) 68

In order to calculate the perimeter of squares and rectangles, you need to use the perimeter formula: (length × 2) + (width × 2)

---

31. If the radius of a circle is 4 and the radians of the subtended angle measure $\pi/4$, what is the length of the arc subtending the central angle?

    A) $\pi/4$

    B) $\pi/8$

    C) π

    D) 4π

Radians can be illustrated by the diagram and formulas that follow.

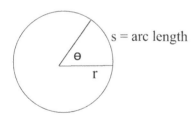

s = arc length

θ = the radians of the subtended angle

s = arc length

r = radius

The following formulas can be used for calculations with radians:

$\theta = s \div r$

$s = r\,\theta$

Also remember these useful formulas.

$\pi \times 2 \times$ radians = 360°

$\pi \times$ radians = 180°

$\pi \div 2 \times$ radians = 90°

$\pi \div 4 \times$ radians = 45°

$\pi \div 6 \times$ radians = 30°

32. A cone has a height of 9 inches and a radius at its base of 4 inches. What is the volume of this cone?
   A) 13π
   B) 24π
   C) 48π
   D) 144π

> Box volume: volume = base × width × height
> Cone volume: (π × radius^2 × height) ÷ 3
> Cylinder volume: π × radius^2 × height
> Sphere volume: 4/3 × π × radius^3

33. If store A is represented by the coordinates (−4, 2) and store B is represented by the coordinates (8,−6), and store A and store B are connected by a line segment, what is the midpoint of this line?
   A) (2, 2)
   B) (2, −2)
   C) (−2, 2)
   D) (−2, −2)

> The midpoint of two points on a two-dimensional graph is calculated by using the midpoint formula: $(x_1 + x_2) \div 2$, $(y_1 + y_2) \div 2$

34. The measurements of a mountain can be placed on a two-dimensional linear graph on which $x = 5$ and $y = 315$. If the line crosses the y axis at 15, what is the slope of this mountain?
   A) 60
   B) 63
   C) 300
   D) 315

> The slope formula: $m = \frac{y_2 - y_1}{x_2 - x_1}$
> The slope-intercept formula: $y = mx + b$, where m is the slope and b is the y intercept.

35. Find x and y intercepts for the following equation: $x^2 + 2y^2 = 144$
   A) $(12, 0)$ and $(0, \sqrt{72})$
   B) $(0, 12)$ and $(\sqrt{72}, 0)$
   C) $(0, \sqrt{72})$ and $(0, 12)$
   D) $(12, 0)$ and $(\sqrt{72} , 0)$

> For questions about x and y intercepts, substitute 0 for y in the equation provided. Then substitute 0 for x to solve the problem.

Trigonometry

36. ∠A measures 58° and cos A = sin B. what is the sum of ∠A + ∠B ?

    A) 15°

    B) 30°

    C) 45°

    D) 90°

Remember these important trigonometric formulas for the exam:

$\cos A = \sin (90° - A)$

$\sin A = \cos (90° - A)$

$\cos^2 A + \sin^2 A = 1$

$\cos^2 A = 1 - \sin^2 A$

$\sin^2 A = 1 - \cos^2 A$

$\tan A = \sin A \div \cos A$

$\tan A \times \cos A = \sin A$

---

37. If x represents a real number, what is the greatest possible value of $4 \times \cos 2x$?

    A) 2

    B) 3

    C) 4

    D) 6

The greatest possible value of cosine is 1. So we can therefore surmise that cos 2x must be less than or equal to 1.

---

38. Use your knowledge of trigonometric functions as you look at the illustration below: $\sin^2 A = ?$

    A) $1 - \cos^2 A$

    B) $\sin^2 A - 1$

    C) $\tan^2 A$

    D) $1 - \tan^2 A$

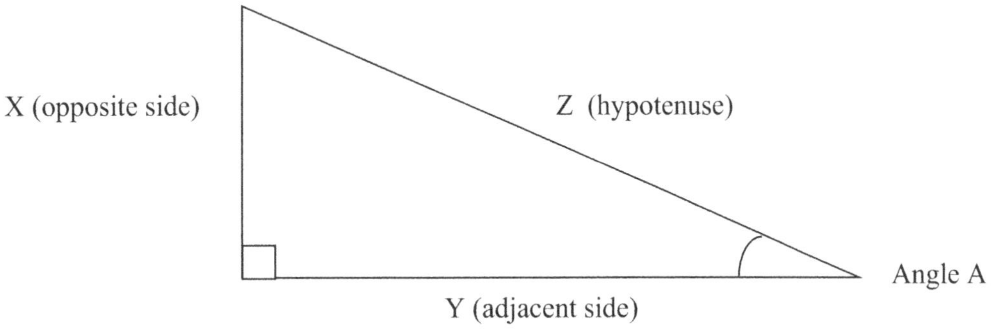

X (opposite side)   Z (hypotenuse)

Angle A

Y (adjacent side)

> To calculate the sine, cosine, and tangent of any given angle A, as in the illustration above:
>
> $$\sin A = \frac{x}{z} = \frac{opposite}{hypotenuse}$$
>
> $$\cos A = \frac{y}{z} = \frac{adjacent}{hypotenuse}$$
>
> $$\tan A = \frac{x}{y} = \frac{opposite}{adjacent}$$

39. If $\cos A = \frac{9}{15}$ and $\tan A = \frac{12}{9}$ then $\sin A = ?$

    A) $\frac{12}{9}$

    B) $\frac{9}{12}$

    C) $\frac{12}{15}$

    D) $\frac{15}{12}$

> We know that $\cos A = \frac{y}{z}$ and $\tan A = \frac{x}{y}$. The facts in our problem state the following:
>
> $\cos A = \frac{9}{15}$ and $\tan A = \frac{12}{9}$

Functions

40. What is the value of $f_1(2)$ where $f_1(x) = 5^x$?
    A) 2^5
    B) 10
    C) 25
    D) 25^2

> This is an example of an exam question involving functions. You may see questions on algebraic, polynomial, exponential, and logarithmic functions on your exam. A function expresses the mathematical relationship between x and y. So, a certain recurring mathematical operation on x will yield the output of y.

Answers to Classic Learning Test Practice Math Exam 1

1) The correct answer is A. Find the perfect squares between 100 and 200 and add 25 to each one:
$10 \times 10 + 25 = 125$
$11 \times 11 + 25 = \mathbf{146}$
$12 \times 12 + 25 = 169$
$13 \times 13 + 25 = 194$
$14 \times 14 + 25 = \mathbf{221}$
$15 \times 15 + 25 = 250$
When we look at these results, we can see that 146 and 221 are the only results that contain two even and one odd digit. So, two numbers satisfy both conditions.

2) The correct answer is A. When we compare the equations, we see that operation Đ is division: the number or variable immediately before Đ is multiplied by 30; and the number or variable immediately after Đ is multiplied by 9. So, the new equation for (3 Đ y) is the following:
$(30 \times 3) \div (9 \times y) = 10$
$(30 \times 3) \div (9 \times y) = 10$
$90 \div 9y = 10$
$y = 1$

3) The correct answer is C. Remember that in order to find the double root of a quadratic, you need to factor the quadratic, and the terms inside each set of parentheses must be identical. The quadratic equation can be expressed in the form $0 = ax^2 + bx + c$. For double roots, the integer represented by variable c in the quadratic equation must be a perfect square, such as 4, 9, 16, 25, and so on. For answer C, we can see that in $y = x^2 + 24x + 144$, variable c is 144, which is a perfect square, so the equation can be factored and expressed as follows: $(x + 12)(x + 12)$. None of the other answer choices can be factored in this way.

4) The correct answer is B. Make a drawing to see if your answer is correct:

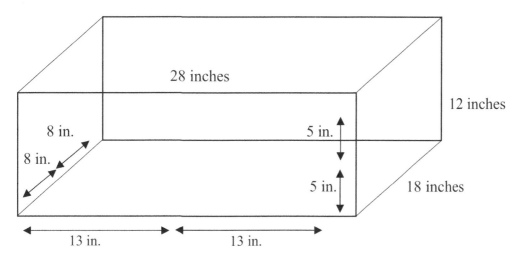

In this way, Susan can fit four shoe boxes flat on the bottom of the container and four more stacked on top of each one of these. Note that Box L would be too small and that Box N would have more empty space in it when the shoe boxes are inside than Box M.

5) The correct answer is D. The facts of the problem state that $x = 6$, so substitute this into the first function:
$g(x) = 2x + 4$
$g(x) = (2 \times 6) + 4$
$g(x) = 16$
So, we are going to input a value of 16 into $f(g(x))$ for an output of 23. The integer 23 is 7 more than 16, so the expression $x + 7$ could be a possible value of $f(x)$.

6) The correct answer is D. Considering the properties of integers provided in the tips following the question, we can see that an even number will result from either the subtraction of two odd numbers or from the subtraction of two even numbers. So, x could be odd or even, and y could be odd or even. Therefore, we cannot choose answer B or answer C. To determine whether x + y could result in a positive integer to check answer A, we need to test the condition stated in the problem, i.e., that $x - y$ is a negative even integer. Here we can insert values to test the premise. For instance, the subtraction of two positives can result in a negative or a positive even integer when subtracted: $5 - 7 = -2$ and $7 - 5 = 2$. Equally, the subtraction of two negatives can result in a negative or a positive even integer when subtracted: $-7 - -1 = -6$ but $-1 - -7 = 6$. Since we cannot determine whether x is positive or negative, nor whether y is positive or negative, we also cannot determine whether x + y could result in a positive integer to check answer A. Accordingly, we must choose "None of the above" as the answer.

7) The correct answer is C. The length of the altitude is 1 more than three times the length of $\overline{YZ}$. Since $\overline{YZ}$ is 6 inches long, the altitude length will be calculated as follows: $(3 \times 6) + 1 = 19$. Then use the Pythagorean theorem to solve: $C = \sqrt{A^2 + B^2}$. See the illustration and solution below.

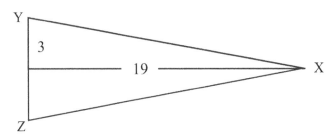

Two triangles are formed when an altitude is drawn, so the base of each right-angled triangle is 3.
$C = \sqrt{A^2 + B^2}$
$C = \sqrt{3^2 + 19^2}$
$C = \sqrt{9 + 361}$
$C = \sqrt{370}$

8) The correct answer is C. Factor the expression first.

$$\left(\frac{6a^2}{3a^{-6}}\right)^3 =$$

$$\left(\frac{6}{3} \times \frac{a^2}{a^{-6}}\right)^3 =$$

$$\left(2 \times \frac{a^2}{a^{-6}}\right)^3$$

Then simplify the exponents inside the parentheses. Remember that you can treat a fraction as division, so subtract the exponents.

$$\left(2 \times \frac{a^2}{a^{-6}}\right)^3 =$$

$$[2 \times (a^{2 - {-6}})]^3 =$$

$$[2 \times (a^8)]^3 =$$

$$(2a^8)^3$$

Finally, perform the operation on the integer and the exponent inside the parentheses by multiplying each one by the exponent outside the parentheses.

$$(2a^8)^3 =$$

$$2^3 a^{(8 \times 3)} = 8a^{24}$$

9) The correct answer is A.
Our inequality is as follows: $10 > |4x - 2|$
To solve, substitute the values from the answer choices into the inequality to see if the result is a true statement.
Let's try answer A, -5:
$20 > |4x - 2|$
$20 > |(4 \times -5) - 2|$
$20 > |(-20 - 2|$
$20 > |-22|$
The absolute value of -22 is 22, which results in the following inequality.
$20 > 22$ is a false statement, so we need to choose A as the answer.
Checking the other answer choices, we can see that we get 0 for answer B, 6 for answer C, and 10 for answer D. All of these are less than 20, so this confirms that A is the right answer.

10) The correct answer is B.
First of all, determine how many watts are equivalent to one amp.
5 amps = 600 watts
1 amp = 600 watts ÷ 5
1 amp = 120 watts
Then multiply this result by the new number of amps to solve. Here we are being asked about 7.5 amps: $120 \times 7.5 = 900$ watts

11) The correct answer is D.
From the formula sheet we can see that $\sin^2 + \cos^2 x = 1$.
So, rearrange the variables in the original equation and solve as follows:
$\sin^2 x + 3 + \cos^2 x =$
$\sin^2 x + \cos^2 x + 3 =$
$1 + 3 = 4$

12) The correct answer is C. We need to calculate the slope of line A. Using the slope formula, we can calculate the slope of line A as follows:

$$\frac{y_2 - y_1}{x_2 - x_1} = \frac{3 - -5}{6 - 2} = \frac{8}{4} = 2$$

The slopes of perpendicular lines are negative reciprocals of each other. So, to get the reciprocal for line B, you need to invert the integer to make a fraction: So, 2 becomes ½. You then need to make this a negative number, so ½ becomes $-$ ½ . Line B has a y intercept of 0 because the facts of the question state that line B passes through the origin (0, 0). Using the slope intercept formula for line B with a slope of $-$ ½ and a y intercept of 0, we get our answer: $y = -\frac{1}{2}x + 0$

13) The correct answer is C. Paul won't sit next to Maria, so answer A is incorrect. Tom won't sit next to Paul, so answer B is incorrect. Jeri has to sit next to Sue, so answer D is incorrect. The arrangement "Paul, Sue, Jeri, Tom, Maria, You" is the only one in which Tom doesn't sit next to Paul, Paul doesn't sit next to Maria, and Jeri is next to Sue.

14) The correct answer is A. The orbits of each of the satellites represent circumference. First, calculate the altitude of Satellite T: $42,178 - 12,647 = 29,531$ km. Then calculate the circumference of satellite T, using the formula for circumference [radius $\times 2 \times 3.14 =$ circumference] and 29,531 for the radius: $29,531 \times 2 \times 3.14 = 185,455$. If it takes satellite S 24 hours to orbit the earth, it travels the distance of 264,878 km at approximately 11,035 km per hour, since $264,878 \div 24 \approx 11,037$. Next, calculate the miles per hour of satellite T: 185,445 km $\div$ 24 hours $\approx$ 7,727 km per hour. Finally, calculate the difference in the speed of the satellites: 11,037 (for satellite S) – 7,727 (for satellite T) = 3,310 km per hour (KPH). So, satellite S travels 3,310 km per hour faster than satellite T. Note that since there is such a large difference between the numbers in the answer choices, in order to save time, you could round the distances up to the nearest thousand when you calculate the KPH.

15) The correct answer is B. Substitute the values from the trigonometric identities on the formula sheet to solve.

$$\frac{\cot A}{\tan A \times \csc A} =$$

$$\frac{1/\tan A}{\sin A / \cos A \times 1/\sin A} =$$

Cancel out sin A in the denominator:

$$\frac{\frac{1}{\tan A}}{\frac{\sin A}{\cos A} \times \frac{1}{\sin A}} =$$

$$\frac{\frac{1}{\tan A}}{\frac{1}{\cos A}}$$

Treat the main fraction as division. Then invert the second fraction and multiply to solve:

$$\frac{\frac{1}{\tan A}}{\frac{1}{\cos A}} = \frac{1}{\tan A} \div \frac{1}{\cos A} = \frac{1}{\tan A} \times \cos A = \frac{\cos A}{\tan A}$$

16) The correct answer is A. Remember that the result of operations inside each set of parentheses is equal to zero for the center of a circle. Our equation is: $(x - 5)^2 + (y - 4)^2$. So, for the left set of parentheses $x = 5$, and for the right set of parentheses $x = 4$. Therefore, the center of the original circle is (5, 4). When a circle is rotated 90 degrees clockwise, the center point does not change. However, when a circle is reflected across the y axis, the sign on the x-coordinate will change from negative to positive or positive to negative. So, when reflected across the y axis (5, 4) becomes (−5, 4).

17) The correct answer is C. First, add the quantity of milliliters together to determine the volume of the new solution: 56 ml + 32 ml = 88 ml. Then determine the relative strength of each solution: 56 × 25% = 14%; 32 × 40% = 12.8%. Then add these together and divide by the new volume to get the strength of the new solution: (14% + 12.8%) ÷ 88 = 26.8% ÷ 88 = 30.45%

18) The correct answer is A. This is a 30°–60°–90° right triangle. One side lies directly on the x axis and has a measure of $\frac{\sqrt{3}}{2}$. The other side lies on the circle and has a height of $\frac{1}{2}$. If we multiply these lengths by 2, we have a similar triangle with side lengths of 1 and $\sqrt{3}$. This means that the proportional length of the hypotenuse of the similar triangle would be 2 because we have a triangle whose side lengths are in the ratio of $1: \sqrt{3}: 2$. According to the rules of similarity, the triangle in our question is also a 30°–60°–90° triangle.

19) The correct answer is C. Real number solutions do not exist for the square root of a negative number. Since a negative number to the power of 3 results in a negative number, our domain or input cannot be a negative number. So, answer A is true. The outputs or range of the function can be both positive or negative since the square root of a positive number can be a positive or negative number. When there are two outputs of y for each input of x, the result will be a parabola. So, answers B and D are true. Since negative values exist for y or the output, answer C is false.

20) The correct answer is A. You need to determine the rate for each person, expressed as the fraction of the job each person can finish in an hour if working alone. The parent needs 20 hours to do the whole job, so he can do 1/20 of the job per hour. The daughter would take 24 hours for the whole job, so she can do 1/24 of the job per hour. The teenage son needs 30 hours to do the whole job,

so he can do 1/30 of the job per hour. To find the combined rate per hour, add up all of the individual hourly rates, after converting them to the common denominator of 120:

$$\frac{1}{20} + \frac{1}{24} + \frac{1}{30} =$$

$$\frac{1 \times 6}{20 \times 6} + \frac{1 \times 5}{24 \times 5} + \frac{1 \times 4}{30 \times 4} =$$

$$\frac{6}{120} + \frac{5}{120} + \frac{4}{120} = \frac{15}{120}$$

Then reduce the fraction, using the common denominator of 15:

$$\frac{15}{120} = \frac{15 \div 15}{120 \div 15} = \frac{1}{8}$$

So, if they all work together, they can get 1/8 of the job done in one hour, meaning that it will take them 8 hours for the whole job if they work together.

21) The correct answer is A. Since the diameter is 3, the circumference of this circle is 3π. The central angle in this problem is 60 degrees. So, here we are dealing with the circumference of $^1/_6$ of the circle since $60 \div 360 = ^1/_6$. Since the arc length is $^1/_6$ of the circumference of the circle, the arc length for this angle is: $3\pi \div 6 = ^\pi/_2$

22) The correct answer is D. You need to determine the number of possible outcomes at the start of the day first of all. The owner has 10 brown teddy bears, 8 white teddy bears, 4 black teddy bears, and 2 pink teddy bears when she opens the attraction at the start of the day. So, at the start of the day, she has 24 teddy bears: $10 + 8 + 4 + 2 = 24$. Then you need to reduce this amount by the quantity of items that have been removed. The problem tells us that she has given out a brown teddy bear, so there are 23 teddy bears left in the sample space: $24 - 1 = 23$. The event is the chance of the selection of a pink teddy bear. We know that there are still two pink teddy bears left after the first prize winner receives his or her prize. Finally, we need to put the event (the number representing the chance of the desired outcome) in the numerator and the number of possible remaining combinations (the sample space) in the denominator. So, the answer is $^2/_{23}$.

23) The correct answer is A. The rule of Pythagorean triples states that the lengths of the three sides of a right-angled triangle can be expressed in the form $a^2 + b^2 = c^2$, with a, b, and c all being integers that are expressed in the ratio: $a: b: c$.

Some examples of Pythagorean triples are as follows:
3: 4: 5
6: 8: 10
5: 12: 13
7: 24: 25

These are just the first four Pythagorean triples, but the quantity of these ratios is infinite. We should try the numbers for the third ratio first because the calculation for the perimeter measurement fits the third ratio: $(5 + 12 + 13) \times 2 = 60$. Then check the calculation for the area measurement. The sum of the areas equals 60 inches, half of which is 30. Taking half of the base length times height, we calculate the area as: $5 \times 12 \div 2 = 30$. So, 5 has to be the correct answer.

24) The correct answer is B. To determine the number of combinations of S at a time that can be made from a set containing N items, you need the formula for combination, which is as follows: $(N!) \div [(N - S)! \times S!]$. In our problem, $S = 2$ and $N = 5$, because there are five toppings available, and the customer selects two of them. When you see the exclamation mark, you are being asked to calculate a factorial, so you need to take the number before the exclamation mark and multiply it by every positive integer less than it. So, substitute the values for S and N to solve.

$(N!) \div [(N - S)! \times S!]$
$(5 \times 4 \times 3 \times 2 \times 1) \div [(5 - 2)! \times (2!)] =$
$(5 \times 4 \times 3 \times 2) \div [(3 \times 2 \times 1) \times (2 \times 1)] =$
$120 \div 12 = 10$

25) The correct answer is D. The entire figure has 12 sides, so divide 108 by 12 to get the length of one side: $108 \div 12 = 9$. Then determine the area of each square. Remember that the area of a square or rectangle is length × width: $9 \times 9 = 81$. The figure consists of five squares, so multiply to solve: $81 \times 5 = 405$ square feet

26) The correct answer is B. For questions on systems of equations with 3 equations, it is usually fastest to substitute the answer choices to see which one is correct, instead of trying to isolate variables in each equation.

For answer B (5, 4, 8), the calculations are as follows.

$\sqrt{b} + c = 2a$
$\sqrt{4} + 8 = 2 \times 5$
$10 = 10$

$c \times {}^a/_b = 10$
$8 \times {}^5/_4 = 10$
${}^{40}/_4 = 10$
$10 = 10$

$2b = 3a - c + 1$
$2 \times 4 = (3 \times 5) - 8 + 1$
$8 = 15 - 8 + 1$
$8 = 8$

We can see that answer B works for each of the three equations. The other answer choices only solve one equation each, not every equation. So, be sure to check the values for each equation in the answer choice when you think you have found the correct answer.

27) The correct answer is B. The angle given in the problem is 90°. If we divide the total of 360° in the circle by the 90° angle, we have: $360 \div 90 = 4$. You can think of arc length as the partial circumference of a circle, so we can visualize that there are 4 such arcs along this circle. We can then multiply the number of arcs by the length of each arc to get the circumference of the circle: $4 \times 8\pi = 32\pi$ (circumference). Finally, use the formula for the circumference of the circle to solve.

Circumference = $\pi \times$ radius $\times 2$
$32\pi = \pi \times$ radius $\times 2$
$32\pi \div 2 = \pi \times$ radius
$16\pi = \pi \times$ radius
$16 =$ radius

28) The correct answer is B.

First of all, isolate x.

$$\frac{x}{5} < -\frac{y}{2} + x$$

$$\frac{x}{5} + \frac{y}{2} < x$$

Find the lowest common denominator.

$$\frac{x}{5} + \frac{y}{2} < x$$

$$\left(\frac{x}{5} \times \frac{2}{2}\right) + \left(\frac{y}{2} \times \frac{5}{5}\right) < x$$

$$\frac{2x}{10} + \frac{5y}{10} < x$$

Then put x on the other side of the equation and reverse the way the inequality points.

$$\frac{2x}{10} + \frac{5y}{10} < x$$

$$x > \frac{2x + 5y}{10}$$

29) The correct answer is C. We know from the facts of the problem that college X admitted 54% of the students (or 54 students) in the previous academic year, so college Y admitted 46% of the students (or 46 students) the same year, since $100 - 54 = 46$. If College Y admitted 50% more of the graduating class in the current academic year than it did the previous academic year, then it admitted 23% more of the students (or 23 more students) in the subsequent year, since $46 \times 50\% = 23$. This means College Y admitted 69% of the students in the current academic year, since $46\% + 23\% = 69\%$, which is more than 50%. So, statements (2) and (3) are true. You may wish to make a table like the one below as you work out the answer to the problem:

College	Previous Year	Current Year
College X	54%	31%
College Y	46%	69%

30) The correct answer is D. The ball travels 200 feet before it bounces the first time. After the first bounce, it will travel 50 feet up, before it falls and travels 50 more feet. So, we are at 300 feet thus far. After the second bounce, the ball will travel 12.5 up and 12.5 feet back down, bringing the total to 325 feet. After the third bounce, it will travel 3.125 up and 3.125 down, for a final total of 331.25 feet, meaning that it has traveled 330 feet before touching the ground the fourth time. So, it has to bounce 3 times to travel 330 feet.

31) The correct answer is C. If a^2 is a positive odd integer, then a can be positive or negative, as long as it is an odd number. This is because two positives when multiplied equal a positive, but the multiplication of two negatives also results in a positive. So, there are two possibilities for $a^b = 1$. For the first, a could be 1 or −1 and b could be greater than zero since, for example, $1^8 = 1$ and $-1^8 = 1$. For the second possibility, b could be 0 and a could be an integer since $a^0 = 1$.

So, let's substitute potential values into the expression ab^{-2}. A negative exponent is equal to its reciprocal, so $ab^{-2} = {}^a/_{b^2}$. In this case, b could not be zero, because the result of b^2 would be zero, and it is impossible to get a real number solution if we divide by zero. Therefore, a could be equal to 1 or −1.

In order to get a whole positive number for ${}^a/_{b^2}$, b cannot be greater than 1; otherwise, the result would be a fraction. Further, a cannot be negative. So, $a = 1$ and $b = 1$, meaning that ab^{-2} is also equal to 1.

32) The correct answer is D. The width is an unknown variable, so we will call this x. The length is 3 more than the width, so we can express the length as $x + 3$, and we know that the area is 40. Hopefully, you may realize intuitively that the container must be 5×8, but for more difficult problems, you can use the following steps to find the solution:

Multiply the length by the width to get the area:
$x(x + 3) = 40$
$x^2 + 3x = 40$

Now express in the quadratic form:
$x^2 + 3x = 40$
$x^2 + 3x - 40 = 0$
Next, you need to factor the equation:
$x^2 + 3x - 40 = 0$
$(x - 5)(x + 8) = 0$
Solve each factor equal for zero:
For $x - 5$, $x = 5$
For $x + 8$, $x = -8$.
Add 3 to the positive value of x to get the length:
$5 + 3 = 8$
So, the base of the container is 5 feet by 8 feet.

To find the volume, we multiply the length of all three sides:
$5 \times 8 \times H = 720$
$H = 720 \div 5 \div 8 = 18$

33) The correct answer is C. First of all, determine the amount of red fabric needed for this order: $2 \times 10 = 20$. Next, find the amount of material needed for each quilt: 2 yards red, 4 yards blue, 1.2 yards gold ($12 \div 10 = 1.2$), and 0.5 yards white $= 2 + 4 + 1.2 + 0.5 = 7.7$ yards each. Then, multiply the total number of quilts by the number of yards per quilt: $10 \times 7.7 = 77$. Finally, divide the amount of red material into the total to solve: $20 \div 77 = 25.97\%$

34) The correct answer is C. In order to create a geometric sequence, each number must be multiplied by a constant in order to get the subsequent number in the series. So, so use inverse operations to solve, remembering that multiplying by a fraction is the same as dividing by the inverted fraction.

$$\frac{3}{10} \times c = -\frac{1}{10}$$
$$c = -\frac{1}{10} \div \frac{3}{10}$$

Then invert the second fraction and multiply.

$$c = -\frac{1}{10} \times \frac{10}{3} = -\frac{10}{30}$$

You can reduce the fraction since both the numerator and denominator are divisible by 10:

$$c = -\frac{10}{30} = -\frac{1}{3}$$

Now check for the next item in the sequence:

$$-\frac{1}{10} \times -\frac{1}{3} = \frac{1}{30}$$

So, the constant is $-\frac{1}{3}$.

35) The correct answer is C. Congruent triangles have three equal angles and three equal sides. It is not enough for all three angles of the two triangles to correspond as the sides of the first triangle could be shorter or longer than the sides of the corresponding triangle. To prove that a triangle is congruent, you need to prove that two corresponding sides and two corresponding angles are congruent. We know from the facts of the problem that $\angle A$ is congruent to $\angle X$ and $\overline{AB} = \overline{XY}$. If we also prove that $\angle C = \angle Z$ and $\overline{AB} = \overline{XZ}$, then we can conclude that the triangles are congruent. So, answer C is correct.

36) The correct answer is A. First, we need to find the circumference of the semicircle on the left side of the figure. The width of the rectangle of 10 inches forms the diameter of the semicircle, so the circumference of an entire circle with a diameter of 10 inches would be 10π inches. We need the circumference for a semicircle only, which is half of a circle, so we need to divide the circumference by 2: $10\pi \div 2 = 5\pi$. Since the right side of the figure is an equilateral triangle, the two sides of the triangle have the same length as the width of the rectangle, so they are 10 inches each. Finally, you need to add up the lengths of all of the sides to get the answer: $18 + 18 + 10 + 10 + 5\pi = 56 + 5\pi$ inches

37) The correct answer is C. First of all, find the surface area of the cube. The surface area of each side of a cube is the side length squared. Here the side length is 4 meters, so the surface area of one side of the cube is 16 square meters, since $4 \times 4 = 16$. There are 6 sides to a cube, so multiply

the surface area of one side by six to get the entire surface area: $16 \times 6 = 96$, so answer A is true. Then, calculate the volume of the entire cube. Since the sphere is inscribed inside the cube, the diameter of the sphere is the same as the side length of the cube. So, the side length of the cube is 4 meters. Substitute this into the formula for the volume of cube: volume = (length of side)^3 = 4^3 = 64 cubic meters. Since the surface area of the cube is 96 square meters and the volume of the entire cube is 64 cubic meters, answer B is also true. Next, find the volume of the sphere. The formula for the volume of the sphere is as follows: volume $\approx 4/3 \times 3.14 \times$ radius^3. We know that radius is always half of diameter, so with a diameter of 4 meters, the radius is 2 meters. So, put this into the formula to find the volume of the sphere: $4/3 \times 3.14 \times$ radius$^3 \approx 4/3 \times 3.14 \times 2^3 \approx$ 33.49 cubic meters. Then, find the volume of the cube that is outside the sphere by subtracting: $64 - 33.49 = 30.51$ cubic meters. So, answer D is also true. Since the volume of the sphere is 33.49 cubic meters and the volume of the cube outside the sphere is 30.51, answer C is false.

38) The correct answer is B. Our equation was $^1/_4x - ^1/_5y = 10$.
First, use inverse operations to isolate y.
$^1/_4x - ^1/_5y = 10$
$^1/_4x = 10 + ^1/_5y$
$^1/_4x - 10 = ^1/_5y$
Then multiply each side by 5 to eliminate the fraction.
$(^1/_4x - 10) \times 5 = ^1/_5y \times 5$
$^5/_4x - 50 = y$
$y = ^5/_4x - 50$

Now we have the equation in the slope-intercept form. The slope-intercept form is as follows: $y = mx + b$, where m is the slope, and b is the y-intercept. Our equation is represented as: $y = ^5/_4x - 50$. The fraction $^5/_4$ is in the position of variable m in the formula, so it is the slope.

39) The correct answer is B. For the point (x, y) on a circle of radius r at an angle of θ like that depicted in the illustration, we can define two important functions as the ratios of the sides of the corresponding triangle: The sine function: $\sin(\theta) = \frac{y}{r} = \frac{4}{5}$. The cosine function: $\cos(\theta) = \frac{x}{r}$. Since we know that the radius of the circle is 5, which is the hypotenuse, and the coordinates of point (x, y) are $(3, 4)$, we can substitute the values into the formulas for the functions as follows:

$$\cos(\theta) = \frac{x}{r} = \frac{3}{5}$$

$$\sin(\theta) = \frac{y}{r} = \frac{4}{5}$$

40) The correct answer is D. Be sure that you are well acquainted with the rules for radians mentioned elsewhere in this book. You should also understand the rules provided in the tip below the question in the practice test.
According to these rules, $\sin\left(\frac{\pi}{2}\right) = 1$
Substituting the value into the equation, we get the following:
$\sin\left(\frac{\pi}{2}\right) = x + 2$
$1 = x + 2$
$1 - 2 = x$
$x = -1$

Answers to Classic Learning Test Practice Math Exam 2

1) The correct answer is B. When point $(6,-1)$ is reflected across the y-axis, the new point is $(-6, -1)$. If point $(10, 3)$ is on the same reflected line, we can calculate the slope as follows:

$$\frac{y_2 - y_1}{x_2 - x_1} =$$

$$\frac{3 - -1}{10 - -6} = \frac{4}{16} = \frac{1}{4}$$

Then we can get the equation of the line from the point-slope formula, using $^1/_4$ for the slope and point $(10, 3)$ as follows:
$$y - y_1 = m(x - x_1)$$

$$y - 3 = {}^1/_4(x - 10)$$

Multiply each side by 4 to get rid of the fraction:

$$y - 3 = {}^1/_4(x - 10)$$

$$(y - 3) \times 4 = [{}^1/_4(x - 10)] \times 4$$

$$4y - 12 = x - 10$$

The standard form of a line is $ax + by = c$, so put the equation in this form to solve:

$$4y - 12 = x - 10$$

$$4y - 12 + 10 = x$$

$$-2 = x - 4y$$

2) The correct answer is C. First of all, express equation $3a = {}^2/_b$ in terms of a.

$$3a = {}^2/_b$$

$$a = {}^2/_b \times {}^1/_3$$

$$a = {}^2/_{3b}$$

Then substitute this value into $3a^3$, being mindful that the operation on the exponents needs to be carried out before the multiplication.

$$3a^3 = 3 \times \left({}^2/_{3b}\right)^3 = 3 \times {}^8/_{27b^3} = {}^{24}/_{27b^3}$$

Finally, simplify the fraction by dividing the numerator and denominator by 3:

$${}^{24}/_{27b^3} = {}^8/_{9b^3}$$

3) The correct answer is C. If door A is locked with the red key, then door B is locked with the blue key. If the key that locks door B also locks door D, then the blue key is also used to lock door D.

4) The correct answer is D. Since the lines are parallel, the unlabeled interior angle of the triangle corresponds to the angle that measures $s - 10°$. In other words, because of the principles of

correspondence and congruency, the unlabeled interior angle of the triangle measures $s - 10°$ as well. Since there are 180° degrees in total when we add up the three angles of any triangle, we can set up and simplify our equation for the triangle as follows:

$180° = s - 10° + s° + 52°$
$180° = 2s° + 42°$
$180° - 42° = 2s°$
$138° = 2s°$
$69 = s°$

Then calculate the measurement of the unlabeled interior angle as follows: 180° in the entire triangle – 52° (from the illustration) – 69° (from our previous calculation) = 59°. Finally calculate the measurement of t: 180° for the straight line – 59° (for the unlabeled interior angle) = 121° = t.

5) The correct answer is B. Find the total of all of the cards at the start: $10 + 15 + 20 + 30 = 75$. The first player received an extra-large card and the second player received a small card, so subtract 2 cards from the previous figure to find out how many cards are left: $75 - 2 = 73$. This number goes in the denominator of the fraction that we are going to make. We want to know the chance of getting a medium card. No medium cards have been handed out at this point, so we still have 20 medium cards left. Put the number of medium cards in the numerator $^{20}/_{73}$. Then divide to find the percentage to solve the problem: $^{20}/_{73} = 27.4\%$

6) The correct answer is A. The store normally has 35 product lines, but is out of three of them since all of its socks, jeans, and t-shirts are out of stock. So, we need to deduct 3 from 35 to get our sample space for the denominator of our fraction. $35 - 3 = 32$. The store chooses two styles of products each day, so there is a chance that these styles could be from the same product line, for example, two different styles of denim jackets. So, we express the probability as a fraction that we convert to a percentage as follows:
$^{2}/_{32} = 2 \div 32 = 0.0625 = 6.25\%$

7) The correct answer is B. We know from the second equation that y is equal to $x + 7$. So put $x + 7$ into the first equation for the value of y to solve.
$-3x - 1 = y$
$-3x - 1 = x + 7$
Then isolate the integers.
$-3x = x + 7 + 1$
Then isolate x.
$-3x - x = 7 + 1$
$-4x = 8$
$-4x \div -4 = 8 \div -4$
$x = -2$

Now we know that the value of x is –2, so we can put that into the equation to solve for y.
$-3x - 1 = y$
$(-3 \times -2) - 1 = y$
$6 - 1 = y$
$y = 5$

8) The correct answer is A. Add the two parts of the ratio together: $7 + 9 = 16$. Then divide this into the total number of books: $128 \div 16 = 8$. Then multiply each part of the ratio by 8 to get the

number of each type of book: 7 × 8 = 56 non-fiction books; 9 × 8 = 72 fiction books. Then subtract the removals and find the new total: 56 – 14 = 42 non-fiction left; 72 – 10 = 62 fiction left; 42 + 62 = 104 total books left. Finally, express the fiction books as a fraction of the total: 62 / 104 = 31 / 52 = 31: 52

9) The correct answer is D. Factor each of the parentheticals in the expression:
$(3x + 3y)(5a + 5b) = 3(x + y) \times 5(a + b)$
We know that $x + y = 5$ and $a + b = 4$, so we can substitute the values for each of the parentheticals: $3(x + y) \times 5(a + b) = 3(5) \times 5(4) = 15 \times 20 = 300$

10) The correct answer is A. The trigonometric function which is needed for this question is:
$\tan A = \sin A \div \cos A$
Substitute the values into the formula to solve. As a shortcut in these kinds of problems, you can round the figures down to two decimal places before you perform the operation.
$\tan A = \sin A \div \cos A$
$\tan A = 0.19 \div 0.98$
$\tan A = 0.194$
Tan A is the same as tan X because the triangles are similar.

11) The correct answer is D. We only need to find the prime numbers between 60 and 90 because any prime number in the nineties will begin with a 9, which is odd. In addition, any prime number in the one-hundreds will begin with a 1, which is odd. The prime numbers between 60 and 90 are as follows: **6**1, **6**7, 71, 73, 79, **8**3, and **8**9. We can see from the highlighted digits that there are four numbers that satisfy the conditions stated in the problem.

12) The correct answer is D. First of all, we need to simplify the equation by canceling out the common factor of 15:
$(d)m = -15m^2 + 30m + 45$
$(d)m = 15(-m^2 + 2m + 3)$

Then set $(d)m$ to zero and divide each side by 15:
$(d)m = 15(-m^2 + 2m + 3)$
$0 = 15(-m^2 + 2m + 3)$
$0 = -m^2 + 2m + 3$

Then multiply each side by –1 and factor the polynomial:
$0 = -m^2 + 2m + 3$
$0 = m^2 - 2m - 3$
$0 = (m + 1)(m - 3)$

To solve, we set each of the parentheticals to zero, leaving us answers of –1 or 3. Since the solution cannot be a negative figure, we know that Martin passes the finish line after 3 minutes.

13) The correct answer is C. Since $m = 0$, the quadratic $ax^2 + bx - c = mx$ can be factored as follows: $(ax - b)(x + c) = 0$. To solve, we need to get either of the parentheticals to be equal to zero. Therefore, two real number solutions exist for the above equation.

14) The correct answer is B. Our coordinates are: (0, 3) and (10, –2). Calculate the slope of the original line using the appropriate formula. The formula for slope is: $^{rise}/_{run} = ^{y_2 - y_1}/_{x_2 - x_1}$
Substitute the values for the coordinates into the slope formula as follows:
$^{-2 - 3}/_{10 - 0} =$
$^{-5}/_{10} =$
$-^1/_2$

The slopes of perpendicular lines are negative reciprocals of each other. So, to get the negative reciprocal the line, you invert the fraction to make an integer and then change the sign from negative to positive. The slope for the perpendicular line is the negative reciprocal of $-^1/_2$, which is 2. Assuming that the perpendicular line passes through the original line at (0, 3), an equation for this perpendicular line is: $y = 2x + 3$

15) The correct answer is D. Go through each answer choice to determine whether it is true or false.
Answer A: Since the three angles of this triangle will have different measurements, the three sides will also have different lengths. Therefore, answer A is true.
Answer B: Since $52° + 38° = 90°$ and since there are 180 degrees in any triangle, the remaining angle must measure 90 degrees, meaning that triangle ABC is a right triangle. So, answer B is true.
Answer C: The length of the hypotenuse of any right triangle will always be greater than the length of either of the other two sides, so answer C is also true.
Answer D: We would need to know the length of at least one of the sides in addition to two of the angles in order to be able to use trigonometric identities. Therefore, answer D is false.

16) The correct answer is C. You need to evaluate the equation in order to determine which operations you need to perform on any new equation containing the operation $\ominus$ and variables x and y. For the special operation $(x \ominus y) = (5x + 2y)$, in any new equation: Operation $\ominus$ is addition; the number or variable before $\ominus$ is multiplied by 5; the number or variable after $\ominus$ is multiplied by 2.
So, the new equation $(6 \ominus y) = 8$ becomes $(6 \times 5) + (y \times 2) = 44$
Now solve.
$(6 \times 5) + (y \times 2) = 44$
$30 + (y \times 2) = 44$
$30 - 30 + (y \times 2) = 44 - 30$
$y \times 2 = 14$
$y = 7$

17) The correct answer is D. The equation for answer D is as follows: $Q^3 – 2$. If we substitute any odd number for Q, we can test the equation. For example, let's substitute 3 for Q: $Q^3 - 2 = 3^3 - 2 = 27 - 2 = 25$. So, answer D is correct. Answer A is incorrect since an odd number times an even number will yield an even number. Answer B is incorrect since raising an odd number to the power of 5 will result in an odd number, and adding 1 to an odd number will yield an even number. Answer C is incorrect since a negative exponent will result in a fraction, not an integer.

18) The correct answer is C. An equilateral triangle has three equal sides and three equal angles. Since all 3 angles in any triangle need to add up to 180 degrees, each angle of an equilateral triangle is 60 degrees $(180° \div 3 = 60°)$. Angles that lie along the same side of a straight line must add up to 180°. So, we calculate angle a as follows: $180° - 60° = 120°$

19) The correct answer is B. To solve, start by isolating the integers to one side of the inequality
$7 - |2x - 5| < 4$
$-|2x - 5| < 4 - 7$
$-|2x - 5| < -3$

Next, since we are making the absolute value negative, we need to check some positive values to find the solution. If we put in 4 for x, we get the following:
$-|2x - 5| < -3$
$-|(2 \times 4) - 5| < -3$
$-|-3| < -3$

Since the value inside the absolute value signs become positive, we get the following:
$-|3| < -3$

This would be correct if we had the equals sign, but we have the less than sign. Next, try 5 for x.
$-|2x - 5| < -3$
$-|(2 \times 5) - 5| < -3$
$-|-5| < -3$
$-|5| < -3$

The above statement is correct, so we have proved that $x > 4$.

Now solve for negative values of the absolute value:
$-(2x - 5) < 3$
$-2x + 5 < 3$
$-2x < 3 - 5$
$-2x < -2$

If we were to put in the number 1 for x, the statement would be correct if we had the equal sign, but we have the less than sign. So, now try to substitute 0:
$-|2x - 5| < -3$
$-|(2 \times 0) - 5| < -3$
$-|-5| < -3$
$-5 < -3$

The above statement is correct, so we have proved that $x < 1$.

So, $x > 4$ and $x < 1$.

20) The correct answer is B. A regular hexagon is made up of six equilateral triangles, as illustrated in drawing below.

Remember that in an equilateral triangle, all three sides are equal. If we draw an altitude in an equilateral triangle in the hexagon, we have a 30°–60°–90° right triangle whose sides are in the ratio of $1 : \sqrt{3} : 2$

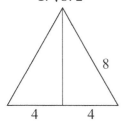

Since the relevant side length in the $1 : \sqrt{3} : 2$ is ratio 2, but our triangle has a side length of 8, we need to multiply the base and height in the original ratio by 4 in order to use them in the triangle formula:

$$\frac{1}{2} \times b \times h =$$

$$\frac{1}{2} \times 8 \times 4\sqrt{3} =$$

$$4 \times 4\sqrt{3} = 16\sqrt{3}$$

We know that there are 6 such the triangles in the hexagon, so the area of the hexagon is:

$$16 \times 6 = 96\sqrt{3}$$

21) The correct answer is A. Simplify the fraction first of all. Remember that the fraction is like division, and that when you divide exponential numbers you need to keep the base the same but subtract the exponents.

$$\frac{10a^2b^4c^5}{5ab^2c^2} = 10a^2b^4c^5 \div 5ab^2c^2 = (10 \div 5)(a^{2-1})(b^{4-2})(c^{5-2}) = 2ab^2c^3$$

Then you need to substitute values from the original equation when $b^2 = a = c^3$ to find the equivalent. Let's try substituting a for b and c first. Since b^2 is equal to a we can substitute a for b^2.

$$2ab^2c^3 = 2a(a)c^3$$

Since c^3 is equal to a we can also substitute a for c^3.

$$2a(a)c^3 = 2a(a)(a) = 2a^3$$

22) The correct answer is C. Use the Pythagorean theorem to test the facts for each answer choice:

$$C = \sqrt{A^2 + B^2}$$

For answer A, side $A = 6$ and side $C = 9$.

$$9 = \sqrt{6^2 + B^2}$$

$$9 = \sqrt{36 + B^2}$$

Then square each side of the equation.

$9 = \sqrt{36 + B^2}$

$9^2 = \sqrt{36 + B^2}^2$

$81 = 36 + B^2$

Then subtract 36 from each side.

$81 = 36 + B^2$

$81 - 36 = B^2$

$45 = B^2$

Finally, find the square root of each side of the equation to solve for B, which is the adjacent side.

$45 = B^2$

$\sqrt{45} = B$

For answer B, side $A = 8$ and side $C = 12$.

$12 = \sqrt{8^2 + B^2}$

$12 = \sqrt{64 + B^2}$

Then square each side of the equation.

$12 = \sqrt{64 + B^2}$

$12^2 = \sqrt{64 + B^2}^2$

$144 = 64 + B^2$

Then subtract 64 from each side.

$144 = 64 + B^2$

$144 - 64 = B^2$

$80 = B^2$

Finally, find the square root of each side of the equation to solve for B.

$80 = B^2$

$\sqrt{80} = B$

For answer C, side $A = 13$ and side $C = 16$.

$16 = \sqrt{13^2 + B^2}$

$16 = \sqrt{169 + B^2}$

Then square each side of the equation.

$16 = \sqrt{169 + B^2}$

$16^2 = \sqrt{169 + B^2}^2$

$256 = 169 + B^2$

Then subtract 169 from each side.

$256 = 169 + B^2$

$256 - 169 = B^2$

$87 = B^2$

Finally, find the square root of each side of the equation to solve for B.

$87 = B^2$

$\sqrt{87} = B$

For answer D, side $A = 5$ and side $C = 10$.

$10 = \sqrt{5^2 + B^2}$

$10 = \sqrt{25 + B^2}$

Then square each side of the equation.

$10 = \sqrt{25 + B^2}$

$10^2 = \sqrt{25 + B^2}^2$

$100 = 25 + B^2$

Then subtract 25 from each side.

$100 = 25 + B^2$

$100 - 25 = B^2$

$75 = B^2$

Finally, find the square root of each side of the equation to solve for B.

$75 = B^2$

$\sqrt{75} = B$

Of these radicals, $\sqrt{87}$ is the largest, so C is the correct answer.

23) The correct answer is A. The graph opens upward, so the equation defining $f(x)$ must have a positive leading coefficient. The graph includes coordinates $(-5, 24)$, $(0, -6)$, and $(6, 24)$, all of which satisfy the equation. The coordinates do not satisfy equation B, and equations C and D have negative leading coefficients, so A is the correct answer.

24) The correct answer is C. The equation $(x + 3)^2 + y^2 = 64$ represents a circle, so the radius of this circle is the square root of 64, which is 8 units. So, put this into the formula for the area of a circle to solve the problem: area $= \pi r^2 = \pi 8^2 = 64\pi$

25) The correct answer is C. XY is the opposite side and XZ is the hypotenuse. Sine is "opposite over hypotenuse", so the sine of angle Z is calculated by dividing XY by XZ.

$\sin z = {}^{XY}/_{XZ} = {}^{opposite}/_{hypotenuse}$

$\sin z = {}^{XY}/_{12}$

Since angle Z is 30 degrees, we can substitute values as follows:

$\sin z = {}^{XY}/_{12}$

$0.5 = {}^{XY}/_{12}$

$0.5 \times 12 = {}^{XY}/_{12} \times 12$

$0.5 \times 12 = XY$

$6 = XY$

26) The correct answer is A. The tower is 15 meters in diameter, so the radius is 7.5. The total circumference of the circle is $2\pi r = 2 \times \pi \times 7.5 = 15\pi$. The area covered with windows relates to 120 degrees and a circle contains 360 degrees, so 240 out of 360 degrees, or 2/3 of the circumference will not be covered with windows. So, multiply 15π by 2/3 to solve:

$15\pi \times {}^{2}/_{3} = {}^{30\pi}/_{3} = 10\pi$

27) The correct answer is C. Convert the side length of the cube to inches: 2 feet + 6 inches = 24 inches + 6 inches = 30 inches. So, the cube is 30 inches long, 30 inches wide, and 30 inches high. Now divide 30 inches by 2.5 inches for each ball: $30 \div 2.5 = 12$ balls. Since each of the sides is 30 inches, we can fit 12 balls by 12 balls on the bottom layer: $12 \times 12 = 144$. We can fit 12 layers in the cube, so multiply by 12 again to solve: $144 \times 12 = 1{,}728$

28) The correct answer is A.
Solve for x in the first inequality:
$-2x - 8 < 30$
$-2x < 30 + 8$
$-2x < 38$
$-2x \div -2 < 38 \div -2$

Remember that you need to reverse the direction the sign points when you divide by a negative number:
$-2x \div -2 < 38 \div -2$
$x > -19$

Now solve for the second inequality:
$x^3 + 12 < 76$
$x^3 < 76 - 12$
$x^3 < 64$
$x < 4$

Now put the two results together for your answer:
$x > -19$ and $x < 4$
$-19 < x < 4$

29) The correct answer is C. The reference of $\frac{1}{\sqrt{2}}$ gives us an 45°–45°–90° degree triangle, whose sides are in the ratio of 1: 1: $\sqrt{2}$. Sine is calculated as "opposite over hypotenuse," meaning that the opposite side is 1 unit in length and the hypotenuse is $\sqrt{2}$. Since tangent is "opposite over hypotenuse, we can then calculate tangent as follows: $\tan = \frac{1}{1} = 1$. We calculate cotangent as $^{1}/_{\tan}$, so cotangent is also 1.

30) The correct answer is C. To solve, you will need to calculate the slope for each answer choice. The formula for slope is:

$$\frac{y_2 - y_1}{x_2 - x_1}$$

Answer A: The points are (–4, 0) and (0, 16)

$$\frac{16 - 0}{0 - -4} = \frac{16}{4} = 4$$

Answer B: The points are (–3, 0) and (4, 14)

$$\frac{14 - 0}{4 - -3} = \frac{14}{7} = 2$$

Answer C: The points are (0, 5) and (9, 7)

$$\frac{7 - 5}{9 - 0} = \frac{2}{9}$$

Answer D: The points are (0, –3) and (1, –11)

$$\frac{11 - -3}{1 - 0} = \frac{14}{1} = 14$$

So, we can see that the line with the smallest slope is that for answer C.

31) The correct answer is D. Go through the answers one by one to check which one is false.
Answer A: We can see from the formula sheet that the surface area of a sphere is $4\pi r^2$ and since the tank is 72 inches in diameter, the radius is 36 inches. Now substitute values to find the surface area: $4\pi r^2 = 4 \times 3.14 \times 36^2 \approx 16{,}278$ cubic inches
Answer B: Calculate in cubic inches the volume of the sphere when it is full. The formula for the volume of a sphere is: $4/3 \times 3.14 \times \text{radius}^3 = 4/3 \times 3.14 \times 36^3 = 195{,}333.12$ cubic inches.
Answer C: We have already determined that the radius is 36 inches.
Answer D: Calculate in cubic inches how much milk remains in the sphere. The tank is now 80% full of milk: 195,333.12 cubic inches × 0.80 = 156,266.50 cubic inches. Answer D transposes the digits 156 to 165, so it is false.

32) The correct answer is A. First of all, determine the RPM of tire R from the facts for tire T. We know that tire T has an RPM 150, so we divide this by 5 from the 5 in the ratio for tire T: $150 \div 5 = 30$. Then multiply this result by 8 to get the RPM for tire R: $30 \times 8 = 240$. Since tire S is 25 percent faster than tire R, get the RPM for tire S by multiplying by 1.25 (100% for tire R + 25% for tire S = 125% = 1.25): $240 \times 1.25 = 300$ RPM for tire S.

33) The correct answer is D. Find the equivalents by substituting the trigonometric identities. Since $\cos^2 \theta + \sin^2 \theta = 1$, it follows by inverse operations that $\cos^2 \theta = 1 - \sin^2 \theta$ and $\sin^2 \theta = 1 - \cos^2 \theta$. Let's look at answer A:

$$2\cos^2 \theta + \frac{1 - \sin^2\theta}{\tan^2\theta} =$$

$$2(1 - \sin^2\theta) + \frac{1 - \sin^2\theta}{\tan^2\theta} =$$

$$2(1 - \sin^2\theta) + \frac{\cos^2\theta}{\tan^2\theta}$$

So, answer A is correct. Now let's consider answer B.

Since $\tan\theta = {\sin\theta}/{\cos\theta}$, then $\tan^2\theta = {\sin^2\theta}/{\cos^2\theta}$, so substitute this value in the denominator of the fraction.

$$2(1 - \sin^2\theta) + \frac{\cos^2\theta}{\tan^2\theta} =$$

$$2(1 - \sin^2\theta) + \frac{\cos^2\theta}{(\sin^2\theta/\cos^2\theta)} =$$

$$2(1 - \sin^2\theta) + \frac{\cos^2\theta}{(\sin^2\theta \div \cos^2\theta)}$$

So, answer B is correct. We go on to evaluate answer C:

Since $\cos^2\theta + \sin^2\theta = 1$, it follows by inverse operations that $\cos^2\theta = 1 - \sin^2$, so substitute this value in the numerator of the fraction.

$$2\cos^2\theta + \frac{\cos^2\theta}{\tan^2\theta} =$$

$$2\cos^2\theta + \frac{1 - \sin^2\theta}{\tan^2\theta} =$$

$$2\cos^2\theta + \frac{1 - \sin^2\theta}{\sin^2\theta / \cos^2\theta} =$$

$$2\cos^2\theta + \left(1 - \sin^2\theta \div \frac{\sin^2}{\cos^2}\right) =$$

$$2\cos^2\theta + \left(1 - \sin^2\theta \times \frac{\cos^2\theta}{\sin^2\theta}\right) =$$

$$2\cos^2\theta + \frac{(1 - \sin^2\theta)\cos^2\theta}{\sin^2\theta}$$

So, answer C is correct. Answer D cannot be derived by substituting any of the identities, so it is incorrect.

34) The correct answer is C. To solve, work backwards from the facts given to calculate the radius of each circle. Circle A has an area of 113.04 inches. So, divide this by 3.14 to determine the calculation of the radius squared: $113.04 \div 3.14 = 36$, so the radius of Circle A is 6. Circle B has a diameter of 20 inches, so its radius is 10 inches. Circle C has an area of 141.3 square inches more than Circle A, so add the areas of the two circles first: $113.04 + 141.3 = 254.34$. Now divide this by 3.14 for π to find R^2: $254.34 \div 3.14 = 81$, so the radius of Circle C is 9. Therefore, Circle A is the least with a radius of 6 inches. Circle C is next, with a radius of 9 inches. Circle B is the greatest with a radius of 10 inches.

35) The correct answer is A. There are no numbers that satisfy condition 1 since any number between 500 and 599 that contains a 3 also contains a 5, making it impossible to have 2 even numbers in any of these 3-digit numbers.

36) The correct answer is C. Our equation was: $y = \frac{5}{2}\cos\left(\frac{x}{4}\right)$. The amplitude is the absolute value of the number before "cos." So, the amplitude is $\frac{5}{2}$. The period of the cos function is 2π. Since the equation in our problem has $\frac{x}{4}$ which equals $x \times \frac{1}{4}$, we need to divide 2π by $\frac{1}{4}$ to get the period of our function: $2\pi \div \frac{1}{4} = 2\pi \times \frac{4}{1} = 8\pi$. So, the amplitude is $\frac{5}{2}$ and the period is 8π.

37) The correct answer is C. Calculate the area of the cylinder at full capacity:
volume = $\pi \times$ (radius)$^2 \times$ height
volume = $\pi \times (3.5)^2 \times 10 = 122.5\pi$ cubic feet

Calculate the area of the cylinder at 55% capacity:
volume = 122.5π cubic feet $\times 0.55 = 67.375\pi$ cubic feet

Divide by 5 and then multiply by 3 to get the amount of drug A in accordance with the ratio:
67.375π cubic feet $\div 5 = 13.475\pi$
$13.475\pi \times 3 = 40.425\pi$

38) The correct answer is B. Notice here that the numerator of the fraction does not change since 1 is equal to 1/1. So, we need to look for the pattern in the denominator. $46 - 27 = 19$; $27 - 12 = 15$; and $12 - 1 = 11$, so our denominators have been reduced by 19, then 15, then 11. Accordingly, the reduction in each denominator in the sequence is 4 less than the previous reduction, and we need to change the denominator of the next fraction by subtracting 4 from 11, which is 7. So, we need to calculate the next fraction in the sequence as follows: $1/(1 - 7)$. Therefore, the next number in the sequence is $-\frac{1}{6}$.

39) The correct answer is C. Two whole numbers that are greater than 1 will always result in a greater number when they are multiplied by each other, rather than when those numbers are divided by each other or subtracted from each other. So, for positive integers, $x \times y$ will always be greater than the following:
$x \div y$
$y \div x$
$x - y$
$y - x$
$1 \div x$
$1 \div y$

40)   The correct answer is C. Toni was able to make a costume very 5 hours, so during the 40 hours working together, she made 8 costumes, while Tom made the remaining 4. This means that it took Tom 10 hours to prepare a single costume, so it will take him 40 more hours to prepare 4 more costumes.

Answers to Classic Learning Test Practice Math Exam 3

1) The correct answer is B. They sell twice as many apples as oranges, so divide the number of apples by two to get the answer: $24 \div 2 = 12$

2) The correct answer is B. We are given the points (0, 2) and (–5, –1) on a parallel line. Use the slope formula to calculate the slope of the original line. The formula for slope is:
$$^{\text{rise}}/_{\text{run}} = ^{y_2 - y_1}/_{x_2 - x_1}$$
Substitute the values for the coordinates:
$$^{-1-2}/_{-5-0}$$
$$^{-3}/_{-5} =$$
$$^3/_5$$
Parallel lines have the same slope, so our equation needs to have $^3/_5$ for the slope. The parallel line passes through the origin (0, 0), so the y-intercept in our equation must be 0. So, the equation for the parallel line is: $y = ^3/_5 x + 0$

3) The correct answer is B. Calculate the rate they can work per minute as a fraction. Fatima gets 1/30 of a car done per minute, while Ashar gets 1/20 of a car done per minute. These two rates, added together, equal the time to wash one car, represented as variable T:
$$\frac{1}{30} + \frac{1}{20} = T$$

Then convert to the common denominator by multiplying the first fraction by 2 and the second fraction by 3:

$$\frac{1}{30} + \frac{1}{20} = T$$

$$\frac{2}{60} + \frac{3}{60} = \frac{5}{60}$$

Then simplify by dividing the numerator and denominator by 5:

$$\frac{5}{60} = \frac{1}{12} = T$$

So, working together they wash $^1/_{12}$ of a car per minute, meaning that it will take them 12 minutes to wash one car if work together. So, multiply to get the time for 5 cars:
5 cars $\times$ 12 minutes per car = 60 minutes = 1 hour

4) The correct answer is A. Multiply the integers, but add the exponents. Remember that any variable times itself is equal to that variable squared. For example, $a \times a = a^2$.
$2ab^2(3ab^3 + 2b) = (2ab^2 \times 3ab^3) + (2ab^2 \times 2b) = 6a^2b^5 + 4ab^3$

5) The correct answer is A. Our figure has 20 sides, so plug this into the formula to solve:
$180(n - 2)° = S$
$180(20 - 2)° = S$
$180(18)° = 3{,}240°$

6) The correct answer is C. The question is asking for numbers that are multiples of 14 from 1 to 200. So, the numbers are as follows: 14, 28, 42, 56, 70, 84, 98, 112, 126, 140, 154, 168, 182, and 196. Therefore, 14 numbers fit the criteria. As a shortcut for these kinds of problems, just try to find the largest multiple, which is this case is 196. We know that $14 \times 14 = 196$, so we can understand that 14 is the answer, without making a list of each and every multiple.

7) The correct answer is D. We have 54 cards in the deck ($13 \times 4 = 52$). We have taken out two spades, one heart, and a club, thereby removing 4 cards. So, the available data set is 48 since $52 - 4 = 48$. The desired outcome is drawing a heart. We have 13 hearts to begin with and one has been removed, so there are 12 hearts left. So, the probability of drawing a heart is:
$^{12}/_{48} = ^{1}/_{4} = 25\%$

8) The correct answer is D. The prism has 5 sides, so we need to calculate the surface area of each one. The rectangle at the bottom of the prism that lies along points, A, B, and D measures 3 units (side AB) by 7 units (side BD), so the surface area of the bottom rectangle is: Length × Width = $3 \times 7 = 21$. Then calculate the area of the rectangle at the back of the triangle, lying along points A and C. This rectangle measures 4 units (side AC) by 7 units (the side that is parallel to side BD). So, the area of this side is: Length × Width = $4 \times 7 = 28$.

Next, we need to find the length of the hypotenuse (side CB). Since AB is 3 units and AC is 4 units, we can use the Pythagorean theorem as follows: $\sqrt{3^2 + 4^2} = \sqrt{9 + 16} = \sqrt{25} = 5$
We can then calculate the surface area of the sloping rectangle that lies along the hypotenuse (along points C, B and D) as: Length × Width = $5 \times 7 = 35$

Next, we need to calculate the surface area of the two triangles on each end of the prism. The formula for the area of a triangle is $bH \div 2$, so substituting the values we get:
$(3 \times 4) \div 2 = 6$

Finally, add the area of all five sides together to get the surface area for the entire prism:
$21 + 28 + 35 + 6 + 6 = 96$

9) The correct answer is B. If $x = -1$, then $x^2 = 1$
$x^3 = x^2 \times x = -1 \times 1 = -1$
$x^4 = x^2 \times x^2 = 1 \times 1 = 1$
So, a pattern emerges: the numbers with odd exponents in the series are equal to -1 and the numbers with even exponents are equal to 1. If we complete the series up to x^{12}, we have the following: $-1 + 1 - 1 + 1 - 1 + 1 - 1 + 1 - 1 + 1 - 1 + 1 = 0$

10) The correct answer is B. Multiply the exponents inside the parentheses by the exponent outside the parentheses. When a variable has no exponent, use 1 for the exponent.
$(a^3 b)^4 =$
$(a^{3 \times 4})(b^{1 \times 4}) =$
$a^{12} b^4$

11) The correct answer is C. There are six sides to the cube, and each side has 9 squares. However, three of these at a minimum need to be beige, so the maximum brown squares on each side is 6. So, multiply 6 brown squares by 6 sides to solve: $6 \times 6 = 36$

12) The correct answer is D.
Factor each of the parentheticals in the expression provided in the problem:
$(4x + 4y)(6a + 6b) =$
$4(x + y) \times 6(a + b)$

We know that $x + y = 5$ and $a + b = 4$, so we can substitute the values stated for each of the parentheticals:
$4(x + y) \times 6(a + b) =$
$4(5) \times 6(4) =$
$20 \times 24 = 480$

13) The correct answer is C. The question is simply asking you to calculate the diameter. The formula for circumference is: Circumference = $\pi \times$ diameter. The diameter is the same as the width, so the diameter is 18 inches: $\pi \times 18 = 18\pi$

14) The correct answer is C. In order to get to 1 from $\frac{3}{5}$, we need to multiply by $\frac{5}{3}$. Carry on with the calculations to determine the missing term: $1 \times \frac{5}{3} = \frac{5}{3}$

Then check the final term of the sequence: $\frac{5}{3} \times \frac{5}{3} = \frac{25}{9}$

15) The correct answer is B. Use the Pythagorean theorem:
$AB^2 + BC^2 = AC^2$
$AB^2 + 8^2 = 10^2$
$AB^2 + 64 = 100$
$AB^2 + 64 - 64 = 100 - 64$
$AB^2 = 36$
$AB = 6$
AB is the adjacent side and BC is the opposite side. Tangent is opposite over adjacent, so the tangent of angle A equals BC divided by AB: $8 \div 6 = {}^{8}/_{6}$. Then simplify to ${}^{4}/_{3}$.

16) The correct answer is D. To solve, substitute the values a = –2 and b = 2 into the expression:
$3^a - 4^b =$
$3^{-2} - 4^2 =$
$3^{-2} - 16$

Remember that a negative exponent becomes a fraction, with 1 in the numerator and the number with the exponent made positive in the denominator.
$3^{-2} - 16 =$

$\frac{1}{3^2} - 16 =$

$\frac{1}{9} - 16$

Express the integer as a mixed number and subtract:

$\frac{1}{9} - 16 =$

$$\frac{1}{9} - 15\frac{9}{9} = -15\frac{8}{9}$$

Then convert the mixed number to an improper fraction to solve:

$$-15\frac{8}{9} = \left(-15 \times \frac{9}{9}\right) - \frac{8}{9} = -\frac{135}{9} - \frac{8}{9} = -\frac{143}{9}$$

17) The correct answer is A. First of all, find the multiples of 13 between 15 and 130. We know that there are going to be nine multiples since $1 \times 13 = 13$, which is less than 15, and $10 \times 13 = 130$, which is the largest multiple in the set. It is usually best to write down the individual multiples if you can. So, the multiples of thirteen between 15 and 130 inclusive are as follows: **26**, 39, **52**, 65, **78**, 91, **104**, 117, and **130**. Then determine which of these multiples are divisible by 2. Of course, every other one of these are even since we get an even number when we add two odd numbers. So, there are 5 multiples of 13 that meet these conditions.

18) The correct answer is B. A parallelogram is a four-sided figure that has two pairs of parallel sides. The opposite or facing sides of a parallelogram are of equal length, and the opposite angles of a parallelogram are of equal measure. You will recall that congruent is another word for equal in measure. So, answer B is correct. A rectangle is a parallelogram with four angles of equal size (all of which are right angles), while a square is a parallelogram with four sides of equal length and four right angles.

19) The correct answer is A. First, we need to calculate the area of the entire triangle: $(9 \times 18) \div 2 = 81$. Then, we need to calculate the base of the shaded portion. Since the height of the shaded portion is 6 and the height of the entire triangle is 18, we know by using the rules of similarity that the ratio of the base of the shaded portion to the base of the entire cone is $^6/_{18}$ or $^1/_3$. Using this fraction, we can calculate the base for the shaded portion. The base of the entire triangle is 9, so the base of the shaded portion is 3: $9 \times ^1/_3 = 3$. Then, calculate the area of the shaded portion: $(3 \times 6) \div 2 = 9$. So, we can express the volume of the shaded portion to the volume of the entire cone as: $^9/_{81}$. We can simplify this to $^1/_9$.

20) The correct answer is C. To solve, set up a table to show how far each car has traveled.

Time	Car C's Distance in miles	Car D's Distance in miles
10:30	25	0
11:00	50	30
11:30	75	60
12:00	100	90
12:30	125	120
1:00	150	150

21) The correct answer is A. For the first step, subtract two of the equations from one another to eliminate z. The second equation has the term $2z$, so multiply the first equation by -2:

$$x + y - z = -1 \quad \longrightarrow \quad -2x - 2y + 2z = 2$$

For the second step, subtract this new equation from the original third equation. Watch the double negatives:

$$x + 3y + 2z = 17$$
$$-(-2x - 2y + 2z = 2)$$
$$\overline{}$$
$$3x + 5y = 15$$

Now isolate x in the second equation:
$x + 3y = 13 \longrightarrow x = 13 - 3y$

Then substitute this value of x in the equation from step 2.
$3x + 5y = 15$
$3(13 - 3y) + 5y = 15$
$39 - 9y + 5y = 15$
$39 - 4y = 15$
$-4y = -24$
$y = 6$

Finally, use 6 for y to solve for x:
$3x + 5y = 15$
$3x + (5 \times 6) = 15$
$3x + 30 = 15$
$3x = -15$
$x = -5$

22) The correct answer is A. When the triangle is rotated $180°$ counterclockwise about the origin, which is point (0, 0), the new triangle is placed in the lower left quadrant, and the coordinates (4, 0) are translated to (–4, 0) in the new triangle. The after the new triangle is reflected, or flipped, across the x-axis, the new triangle is placed in the upper left quadrant and point (–4, 0) remains at point (–4, 0).

23) The correct answer is D. First, calculate the area of the central rectangle. The area of a rectangle is length times height: $8 \times 3 = 24$. Then we use the Pythagorean theorem to work out that the base of each triangle is 4.
$5 = \sqrt{3^2 + base^2}$
$5^2 = 3^2 + base^2$
$25 = 9 + base^2$
$25 - 9 = base^2$
$16 = base^2$
$4 = base$
Then calculate the area of each of the triangles on each side of the central rectangle. The area of a triangle is base times height divided by 2: $(4 \times 3) \div 2 = 6$. So, the total area for the trapezoid is the area of the main rectangle plus the area of each of the two triangles: $24 + 6 + 6 = 36$

24) The correct answer is B. The ratio of the bases of the figures to one another is $^6/_{10}$. Because the two figures are similar, we can use this ratio to find the lengths of the other sides of KLMN. The length of $\overline{KM}$ and $\overline{LM}$ is as follows: $6 \times {}^6/_{10} = 3.6$. Then find the length of $\overline{KL}$ by multiplying

by 8 by the ratio: $8 \times {}^{6}/_{10} = 4.8$. Then add the lengths of all of the sides to find the perimeter: $6 + 3.6 + 3.6 + 4.8 = 18$ inches

25) The correct answer is B. This question is asking you to find counter-examples to a statement by using basic operations. First of all, rule out all answer choices that include a factor that is the same as the divisor stated in the facts of the question. Answers C and D multiply another number by 6. These factors of 6 are of course divisible by 6, which supports the statement above instead of disproving it. Answer A is irrelevant since the product is not divisible by 6. Answer B disproves the statement because 12 is divisible by 6, although neither 3 nor 4 is divisible by 6.

26) The correct answer is C. The range is calculated by subtracting the lowest value from the highest value. So, the range is $8 - 1 = 7$. Then add up the individual values from each line to calculate the mean of each of the answer options. The mean is the average of all of the numbers in the set. If we look at each of the answers, we can see that we have seven values in each set because there are seven dots above each of the number lines. The mean for answer choice C is 4.57 and the median is 5. Mean: $1 + 2 + 3 + 5 + 6 + 7 + 8 = 32$; $32 \div 7 = 4.57$. The median is the middle value in a data set when the values are in ascending order. Accordingly, the median is: 1, 2, 3, **5**, 6, 7, 8. So, the range exceeds the median, and the median exceeds the mean for the set represented on number line (C).

27) The correct answer is B. The smallest multiple of 8 that meets condition 1 is 200 because $8 \times 25 = 200$. The largest multiple of 8 that meets condition 1 is 696, since $8 \times 87 = 696$. Excluding 8, the other factors for the appropriate numbers that meet condition 1 range from 25 to 87 inclusive, so 63 integers meet condition 1. Since 8 and 9 do not have a common factor, we can exclude multiples of 72 between 200 and 692 for condition 2. The largest and smallest multiples of 72 in our set are as follows: $72 \times 3 = 216$ and $72 \times 9 = 648$. These factors range from 3 to 9 inclusive, so there are 7 multiples of 72 to exclude. To find how many integers meet both conditions, we subtract 7 from 63: $63 - 7 = 56$

28) The correct answer is D. In order to use the least amount of space, the javelin need to be placed with one end in a lower corner and the other end in the upper corner on the opposite side. To calculate this length, we first need to determine the diagonal distance across the base of the box, using the Pythagorean Theorem.

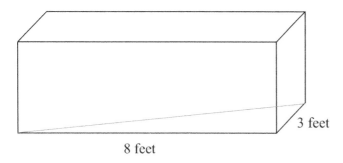

8 feet

$C = \sqrt{A^2 + B^2}$

$C = \sqrt{3^2 + 8^2}$

$$C = \sqrt{9 + 64}$$

$$C = \sqrt{73}$$

Then use this length to determine the upper-to-lower diagonal:

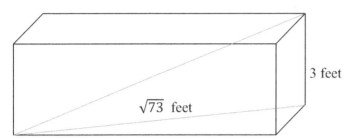

$$C = \sqrt{A^2 + B^2}$$

$$C = \sqrt{3^2 + \sqrt{73}^2}$$

$$C = \sqrt{9 + 73}$$

$$C = \sqrt{82}$$

$$C \approx 9$$

29) The correct answer is B. The original function from the question has an amplitude of 1, so multiplying it by 2 will yield an amplitude of 2. The period of sine is calculated as $\frac{2\pi}{|b|}$, so we need to solve for b in this equation with respect to the period. We know that our period is $\frac{\pi}{2}$, so set up the following equality:

$$\frac{2\pi}{|b|} = \frac{\pi}{2}$$

$$\frac{2\pi}{|4|} = \frac{\pi}{2}$$

In other words, $b = 4$.

We need to put the value of b after "sin" in the equation for our answer.

So, the correct answer is $y = 2 \sin 4\theta$.

30) The correct answer is C. Calculate the volume of the display case first:
The radius of the display case is: 1,280 mm diameter ÷ 2 = 640 mm
volume = 4/3 × π × radius³
volume = 4/3 × π × 640³
volume ≈ 349,525,333π mm

Calculate how many balls can be suspended across the diameter of the case:
$1{,}280 \div 40 = 32$

Calculate the volume of one golf ball:
The radius of each golf ball is: 40 mm diameter $\div\, 2 = 20$ mm
volume $= 4/3 \times \pi \times 20^3$
volume $\approx 10{,}667\pi$ mm

Calculate the volume of all 32 balls:
$10{,}667\,\pi$ mm $\times\, 32 \approx 341{,}333\pi$ mm

Calculate the difference between the total volume of the case and the volume of the 32 golf balls.
(Note that the volume of the fishing line is not included since the volume is approximate.)
$349{,}525{,}333\pi$ mm $- 341{,}333\pi$ mm $= 349{,}184{,}000\pi$ mm

31)   The correct answer is B. The point or points of intersection will be found at the following
equation: $-x^2 + 6x - 6.5 = x^2 - 2$

We need to set the left side of the equation to zero:
$-x^2 + 6x - 6.5 = x^2 - 2$
$0 = 2x^2 - 6x + 4.5$

Use the quadratic formula to solve:
$$x = \frac{-b \pm \sqrt{b^2 - 4ac}}{2a}$$

In our equation $0 = 2x^2 - 6x + 4.5$, $a = 2$, $b = -6$, and $c = 4.5$

$$x = \frac{6 \pm \sqrt{6^2 - (4 \times 2 \times 4.5)}}{2 \times 2}$$

$$x = \frac{6 \pm \sqrt{36 - 36}}{4}$$

$$x = 1.5$$

Since the square root of 0 is 0, we will have only one point of intersection.

Then substitute the value of x into one of the original equations to solve for y:
$x^2 - 2 = y$
$1.5^2 - 2 = y$
$0.25 = y$

32)   The correct answer is A. $\tan A = \sin A \div \cos A$, so substitute the values into the appropriate
formula: $\tan A = \sin A \div \cos A$
$\tan A = 0.95106 \div 0.30902$
$\tan A = 3.07767$

33) The correct answer is C. Divide by the fractional hour in order to determine the speed for an entire hour: 38.4 miles ÷ $^4/_5$ of an hour = 38.4 × $^5/_4$ = (38 × 5) ÷ 4 = 48 mph

34) The correct answer is C. The length of arc PQ is 4π units, so first multiply by 3.14 to eliminate π: 4 × 3.14 = 12.56. Then determine what part of the circumference of the circle we are dealing with. The two rays form a 32° angle, and there are 360° in a circle, so we divide to show that 360 ÷ 32 = 11.25, meaning that there are $11^1/_4$ such arcs that form the circumference of this circle. In other words, the length of one arc is $^1/_{11.25}$ of the circumference. So, multiply the length of the arc by 11.25 to get the circumference: 12.56 × 11.25 = 141.3 units. Therefore, answer B is true. Since circumference is equal to π times diameter, and we are using 3.14 for π, we can divide the circumference by 3.14 to get the diameter: 141.3 units ÷ 3.14 = 45 units, meaning that answer A is true. Then divide the diameter by 2 to get the radius: 45 ÷ 2 = 22.5 units. Accordingly, answer D is true. Finally calculate the area to check your answer. 22.5^2 × 3.14 ≈ 1,590 units. So, answer C is false.

35) The correct answer is A. Since the greatest possible value of sine is 1, sine $2x$ must be less than or equal to 1. So, the greatest possible value of sin $2x$ is represented as sin $2x = 1$.
Multiply each side of this equation by 8:
sin $2x$ × 8 = 1 × 8
So, the greatest possible value is 8.

36) The correct answer is B. First of all, calculate the sum of the digits of all of the answer choices.
A) 5
B) 1 + 5 = 6
C) 3 + 2 = 5
D) 6 + 4 = 10

Then find the factors of each of the answer choices:
A) 5 = 1 × 5 (2 factors)
B) 15 = 1 × 15 and 3 × 5 (4 factors)
C) 32 = 1 × 32; 2 × 16; 4 × 8 (6 factors)
D) 64 = 1 × 64; 2 × 32; 4 × 16; 8 × 8 (8 is repeated, so there are 7 distinct factors.)

Then compare the number of factors to the sum of the digits:
A) sum = 5; 2 factors; difference = 3
B) sum = 6; 4 factors; difference = 2
C) sum = 5; 6 factors; difference = 1
D) sum = 10; 7 factors; difference = 3
The condition states that the sum of the digits is 2 more than the number of distinct individual factors, so B is the correct answer.

37) The correct answer is A. First of all, divide the octagon into a central square, 4 rectangles, and 4 triangles as shown below. (The drawing is not to scale.)

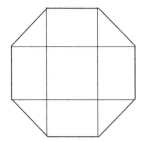

Since the triangles are right triangles and have a side length of $5\sqrt{2}$ inches, we know that we are dealing with a 45–45–90 triangle. The lengths of the sides of any 45°–45°–90° triangle will be in the ratio of $1: 1: \sqrt{2}$. So, the hypotenuse of each of the triangles is $5\sqrt{2}$ inches and the other sides each have a length of 5 inches since the ratio $5: 5: 5\sqrt{2}$ is equal to the ratio of $1: 1: \sqrt{2}$.

Accordingly, the area of each of the triangles is calculated as:

(base × height) $\div 2 = (5 \times 5) \div 2 = \dfrac{25}{2}$

There are four such triangles in our figure, so the total area of all four triangles is:

$\dfrac{25}{2} \times 4 = 50$

The area of each of the rectangles is calculated as length × width. According to the ratio, our length is $5\sqrt{2}$ and our width is 5: $5\sqrt{2} \times 5 = 25\sqrt{2}$

There are four such rectangles in our figure, so the total area of all four rectangles is:

$25\sqrt{2} \times 4 = 100\sqrt{2}$

We also need to calculate the area of the central square, which has a side length of $5\sqrt{2}$:

$5\sqrt{2} \times 5\sqrt{2} = 25 \times 2 = 50$

Now add up all of the areas to solve:

$50 + 100\sqrt{2} + 50 = 100\sqrt{2} + 100$ square inches

38) The correct answer is A. We know that 2 inches represents F feet. We can set this up as a ratio $2/F$. Next, we need to calculate the ratio for $F + 1$. The number of inches that represents $F + 1$ is unknown, so we will refer to this unknown as x.
So, we have:

$\dfrac{2}{F} = \dfrac{x}{F + 1}$

Now cross multiply.

$\dfrac{2}{F} = \dfrac{x}{F + 1}$

$F \times x = 2 \times (F + 1)$

$Fx = 2(F + 1)$

Then isolate x to solve.

$Fx \div F = [2(F + 1)] \div F$

$x = \dfrac{2(F + 1)}{F}$

39) The correct answer is D. Do not be tempted to subtract the radii and then put this difference into the circle area formula. You need to calculate the area of each circle and then subtract these two results. The formula for the area of a circle is: πR^2. The area of circle A is $\pi \times 5^2 = 25\pi$ and the area of circle B is $\pi \times 3^2 = 9\pi$. So, the difference between the areas is 16π. The formula for circumference is: $\pi 2R$. The circumference of circle A is $\pi \times 2 \times 5 = 10\pi$ and the circumference for circle B is $\pi \times 2 \times 3 = 6\pi$. The difference in the circumferences is 4π. So, answer D is correct.

40) The correct answer is C. This is a question about radians. Remember these rules:
$\pi \times 2 \times \text{radian} = 360°$
$\pi \times \text{radian} = 180°$
$\pi \div 2 \times \text{radian} = 90°$
$\pi \div 4 \times \text{radian} = 45°$
$\pi \div 6 \times \text{radian} = 30°$

We can see that the rotation is less than 180° counterclockwise, but more than 180° clockwise. Since answer choices A and B are less than $\pi \times$ radian or 180°, we can rule them out as they are incorrect answers. In addition, answer D is more than 180° counterclockwise, so it is also incorrect. By looking at the illustration, we can see that the rotation is approximately $90° + 60°$ counterclockwise. So, using the rules $\pi \div 2 \times \text{radians} = 90°$ and $\pi \div 6 \times \text{radians} = 30°$, we can calculate the counterclockwise rotation as follows:

$(\pi \div 2) + (\pi \div 6) + (\pi \div 6) \text{ radian} =$

$\dfrac{\pi}{2} + \dfrac{\pi}{6} + \dfrac{\pi}{6} \text{ radian} =$

$\dfrac{3\pi}{6} + \dfrac{\pi}{6} + \dfrac{\pi}{6} \text{ radian} = \dfrac{5\pi}{6} \text{ radian}$

As stated previously, the rotation is counterclockwise.

Answers to Classic Learning Test Practice Math Exam 4

1) The correct answer is D.
    In our function $x = 2$, so put in the value of 2 for x in the function:
    $49^{1/x} =$
    $49^{1/2}$
    A number to the power of one-half is the same as the square root of the number.
    $49^{1/x} = \sqrt{49} = \sqrt{7 \times 7} = 7$

2) The correct answer is B. Remember that the range is the output, or the value of y, for a function. Any positive or negative number to the power of four will result in a positive number. When x^4 is multiplied by –5, the product will always be negative, except when x is equal to zero. When $x = 0$, the result is –8. So, the range is: $y \le -8$.

3) The correct answer is A. Multiply the numerator of the first fraction by the numerator of the second fraction to get the new numerator. Then multiply the denominators.
    $$\frac{3a^2}{4} \times \frac{2}{a^3} =$$
    $$\frac{3a^2 \times 2}{4 \times a^3} =$$
    $$\frac{6a^2}{4a^3}$$

    Then find the greatest common factor and cancel out to simplify.
    $$\frac{6a^2}{4a^3}$$
    $$\frac{2 \times 3 \times a \times a}{2 \times 2 \times a \times a \times a} =$$
    $$\frac{\cancel{2} \times 3 \times \cancel{a} \times \cancel{a}}{\cancel{2} \times 2 \times \cancel{a} \times \cancel{a} \times a} = \frac{3}{2a}$$

4) The correct answer is C. To carry out the "complete the square" method, we need to express the equation in the quadratic form and identify the variables.
    First, expand the equation to identify variables b and c.
    Our equation $x^2 - 8x + 1 = 0$ is in the format $x^2 + 2bx + c$.
    $x^2 + (2 \times -4 \times x) + 1 = x^2 + 2bx + c$
    So, $b = -4$ and $c = 1$

    Then put the equation in the following format: $(x + b)^2 - b^2 + c$
    $(x - 4)^2 - (-4)^2 + 1$

    Next perform the operations to simplify.
    $(x - 4)^2 - (-4)^2 + 1 = 0$
    $(x - 4)^2 - 16 + 1 = 0$

$(x - 4)^2 - 15 = 0$
$(x - 4)^2 = 0 + 15$
$(x - 4)^2 = 15$

Finally, take the square root of each side and simplify to solve.

$(x - 4)^2 = 15$

$\sqrt{(x - 4)^2} = \pm\sqrt{15}$

$x - 4 = \pm\sqrt{15}$

$x = \pm\sqrt{15} + 4$

5) The correct answer is A. If classes last for 45 minutes and there are 4 classes before lunch, the morning classes last for 3 hours in total. If lunch is at 12:30, it is therefore possible for classes to begin at 9:30.

6) The correct answer is B.
Isolate the integers to the left side of the inequality to get 0 on the right:
$x^2 - 11x < -24$
$x^2 - 11x + 24 < -24 + 24$
$x^2 - 11x + 24 < 0$
When you have the quadratic in this form, you can factor it.
The factors of 24 are: 1×24, 2×12, 3×8, and 4×6.
We need to find the two factors that add up to -11, so we need -3 and -8.
Then express the inequality as a factored quadratic:
$(x - 3)(x - 8) < 0$
Then find the values of x that satisfy the quadratic. You do this by putting in zero for the x in each set of parentheses.
$(x - 3)(x - 8) < 0$
$(0 - 3)(x - 8) < 0$
$x < 8$

$(x - 3)(x - 8) < 0$
$(x - 3)(0 - 8) < 0$
$3 < x$
Then express in an inequality to solve:
$3 < x < 8$

7) The correct answer is D. Functions have one output value for each input value. So, for each value of x, a function will yield a corresponding value of y. Moreover, two different inputs can yield the same output, such a positive and negative values of an integer squared. Graphs A, B, and C have more than one corresponding value of y for certain values of x, so they are not functions.

8) The correct answer is C. If each number in the set is increased by 2, the mean will increase by 2. Here we have 9 numbers in the set, so the overall increase in the total of the values ($2 \times 9 = 18$) will be divided equally among all nine items in the set ($18 \div 9 = 2$) when the mean is calculated. Since each of the numbers increases by 2, the median number will also increase by 2. So, both the median and mean will be greater than before.

9)   The correct answer is B. First, we will use variable T as the total number of items in the set. The probability of getting a red scarf is $^1/_3$. So, set up an equation to find the total items in the data set:

$$\frac{5}{T} = \frac{1}{3}$$

$$\frac{5}{T} \times 3 = \frac{1}{3} \times 3$$

$$\frac{5}{T} \times 3 = 1$$

$$\frac{15}{T} = 1$$

$$15 = T$$

We have 5 red scarves, 6 blue scarves, and x green scarves in the data set that make up the total sample space, so now subtract the number of red and blue scarves from the total in order to determine the number of green scarves.

$5 + 6 + x = 15$

$11 + x = 15$

$x = 15 - 11$

$x = 4$

10) The correct answer is D. The perimeter is the measurement along the outside edges of a rectangle or other area. The formula for perimeter is as follows: P = 2W + 2L. The room is 12 feet by 10 feet, and each piece is 18 inches or 1.5 feet long, so for the two length-wise sides of the room we need: (12 ÷ 1.5 feet) × 2 = 16 pieces. Then for one of the width-wise sides of the room we need (10 ÷ 1.5 feet) = 6.7, which we round up to 7 pieces. Next subtract the amount for the door from one side. We will do this calculation in inches: (120 inches – 35 inches) ÷ 18 inches per piece = 4.7, which we round up to 5 pieces. Then, we need to add up the number of pieces for all four sides: 16 + 7 + 5 = 28 pieces. You may be tempted to add the widths together, subtract the door width, and then divide, but this would create more joints.

11) The correct answer is C. To solve, set up a rational expression with the equation for KE in both the numerator and denominator. The mass of the pear is double that of the apple, and the velocity of the pear is ¼ more than that of the apple, in other words 5/4 times the apple. So, substitute the values for the pear into the denominator of the fraction and simplify the expression as shown:

$$\frac{\frac{1}{2}m_1 v^2}{\frac{1}{2}m_2 v^2} =$$

$$\frac{\frac{1}{2}m_1 v^2}{\frac{1}{2}(2m_1)\left(\frac{5}{4}v\right)^2} =$$

$$\frac{\frac{1}{2}m_1 v^2}{\left(\frac{5}{4}\right)^2 m_1 v^2} =$$

$$\frac{\frac{1}{2}}{\left(\frac{5}{4}\right)^2}$$

Then invert and multiply:

$$\frac{\frac{1}{2}}{\frac{25}{16}} =$$

$$\frac{1}{2} \div \frac{25}{16} =$$

$$\frac{1}{2} \times \frac{16}{25} = \frac{16}{50}$$

Simplify by dividing the numerator and denominator by the common factor of 2:

$$\frac{16}{50} = \frac{8}{25}$$

12) The correct answer is C. The formula for circumference is: $\pi \times 2 \times R$. The center of the circle is on (0, 0) and the radius of the circle is 3. Therefore, the circumference is: $\pi \times 2 \times 3 = 6\pi$

13) The correct answer is C. If we take a negative even number to the power of 3, the result is a negative even number. For example, $-4 \times -4 \times -4 = -64$. So, y is a negative even integer. In order to get a negative integer when we add another integer to this, we can add either a positive or negative even or odd integer. So, we can surmise that x is either a positive or negative even or odd integer. With respect to finding the value of xy, bear in mind that when we multiply any integer by an even number, we will get an even number as the result. And when we multiply a negative integer by a positive integer, the result will be a negative integer. But when we multiply a negative integer by a negative integer, the result will be a positive integer. So, xy will be a positive or negative even integer.

14) The correct answer is B. We need to calculate sin Z, so we need the formula: opposite/hypotenuse. From the facts of the problem, we know that this is $^{XY}/_{YZ}$. XY is 9 units long and side YZ is 15 units long, so substitute the length provided for each side to solve: $^{9}/_{15}$

15) The correct answer is A. No real numbers exist for negative square roots, so the answer is 0.

16) The correct answer is C. Our equation is $x^2 + y^2 = 9$. Our circle is centered around the origin and has a radius of 3 since $\sqrt{9} = 3$. So, the horizontal tangent lines pass over the top and bottom of the circle at (0, 3) and (0, –3). The vertical tangent lines pass on the left and right sides of the circle, and intersect it at (–3, 0) and (3, 0).

The four quadrants of the *xy*-coordinate plane are as follows:

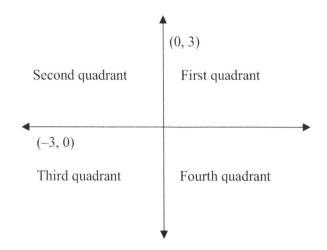

So, we have four points of tangency: (0, 3), (0, –3), (–3, 0) and (3, 0). However, we need to find the points that lie on the axes between the first and second quadrants and the second and third quadrants. So, our answers are (0, 3) and (–3, 0).

17) The correct answer is C. Count the edges of the gray blocks, rather than the blocks themselves to solve. Top boundary = 4 edges. Left boundary = 7 edges. Bottom boundary = 3 edges. Right boundary = 8 edges. Then add these amounts together and multiply by 4 to get your result: $4 + 7 + 3 + 8 = 22 \times 4$ feet each = 88 feet

18) The correct answer is D. The formula for the area of a circle is: $\pi \times R^2$. First, we need to calculate the area of the larger circle: $\pi \times 2.4^2 = 5.76\pi$. Then calculate the area of the smaller inner circle: $\pi \times 1^2 = \pi$. We need to find the difference between half of each circle, so divide the area of each circle by 2 and then subtract.

$$(5.76\pi \div 2) - (\pi \div 2) = \frac{5.76\pi}{2} - \frac{\pi}{2} = \frac{4.76\pi}{2} = 2.38\pi$$

19) The correct answer is D. The slope intercept formula is: $y = mx + b$. Remember that m is the slope and b is the y intercept. You will also need the slope formula: $m = \dfrac{y_2 - y_1}{x_2 - x_1}$

We are given the slope, as well as point (4,5), so first we need to put those points into the slope formula. We are doing this in order to solve for b, which is not provided in the facts of the problem.

$$\frac{y_2 - y_1}{x_2 - x_1} = -\frac{3}{5}$$

$$\frac{5 - y_1}{4 - x_1} = -\frac{3}{5}$$

Then eliminate the denominator.

$$(4 - x_1)\frac{5 - y_1}{4 - x_1} = -\frac{3}{5}(4 - x_1)$$

$$5 - y_1 = -\frac{3}{5}(4 - x_1)$$

Now put in 0 for x_1 in the slope formula in order to find b, which is the y intercept (the point at which the line crosses the y axis).

$$5 - y_1 = -\frac{3}{5}(4 - x_1)$$

$$5 - y_1 = -\frac{3}{5}(4 - 0)$$

$$5 - y_1 = -\frac{3 \times 4}{5}$$

$$5 - y_1 = -\frac{12}{5}$$

$$-y_1 = -\frac{12}{5} - 5$$

Now make the negatives positive by multiplying both sides by –1.

$$-y_1 = -\frac{12}{5} - 5$$

$$-y_1 \times -1 = \left(-\frac{12}{5} - 5\right) \times -1$$

$$y_1 = \frac{12}{5} + 5$$

Next, convert to an improper fraction.

$$y_1 = \frac{12}{5} + \left(5 \times \frac{5}{5}\right)$$

$$y_1 = \frac{12}{5} + \frac{25}{5}$$

$$y_1 = \frac{37}{5}$$

Remember that the y intercept (known in the slope-intercept formula as the variable b) exists when x is equal to 0. We have put in the value of 0 for x in the equation above, so $b = \dfrac{37}{5}$. Now put the value for b into the slope intercept formula: $y = mx + b$

$$y = -\frac{3}{5}x + \frac{37}{5}$$

20) The correct answer is D. Substitute the values from each of the answer choices into the equations to solve, rather than trying to eliminate variables. We can easily eliminate answer choices A and C, because when $x = 2$ in the third equation, $z = 1/3$, which results in an integer with a fraction, and all of our equations result in an integer value.

So, let's look at answer choice B. If we substitute -12 for x, we can see that the equation is going to result in a negative value.

Therefore, answer D must be the correct answer. So, check the values provided in answer D for all three equations. The values in answer D are as follows: $x = 12$, $y = -16$, and $z = 2$.

The first equation is:
$6x + 3y + z = 26$
$6x + 3y + 2 = 26$
$(6 \times 12) + (3 \times -16) + 2 = 26$
$72 - 48 + 2 = 26$
$26 = 26$

The second equation is:
$10x + 6y + 3z = 30$
$(10 \times 12) + (6 \times -16) + 3(2) = 30$
$120 - 96 + 6 = 30$
$30 = 30$

The third equation is:
$x \div 6 = z$
$12 \div 6 = 2$
$2 = 2$

So, we have proved that D is the correct answer.

21) The correct answer is C. One radian is the measurement of an angle at the center of a circle which is subtended by an arc that is equal in length to the radius of the circle.
These symbols are used in questions on radians:
θ = the radians of the subtended angle
s = arc length
r = radius
The following formulas can be used for calculations with radians:
$\theta = s \div r$
$s = r\,\theta$
Use the second formula from above, and substitute values to solve the problem.
In our problem:
radius (r) = 3
radians (θ) = $^\pi/_3$
$s = r\,\theta$
$s = 3 \times {}^\pi/_3$
$s = \pi$

22) The correct answer is D. The line $x = -2$ is vertical and parallel to the *y*-axis. So, the point of intersection with the circle also needs to have an *x*-coordinate of -2. Coordinates $(-2, 0)$ meet these criteria.

23) The correct answer is A. The circular plane is perpendicular to the base of the cylinder, so a right angle is formed. Therefore, the perpendicular circular plane would need to be equal or lesser in size to the bottom of the cylinder in order for it to fit inside the cylinder. So, the radius of the perpendicular circular plane would need to be equal to or less than the radius of the base of the cylinder. Therefore, the radius of the perpendicular cylinder could be equal to R.

24) The correct answer is D. The area of a circle is always π times the radius squared. Therefore, the area of circle A is: $3^2\pi = 9\pi$. Since the circles are internally tangent, the radius of circle B is calculated by taking the radius of circle A times 2. In other words, the diameter of circle A is the radius of circle B. Therefore, the radius of circle B is $3 \times 2 = 6$ and the area of circle B is $6^2\pi = 36\pi$. To calculate the remaining area of circle B, we subtract as follows: $36\pi - 9\pi = 27\pi$

25) The correct answer is B. Our series was:

$$\frac{1}{4}, \frac{5}{8}, \frac{9}{12}, \frac{13}{16}$$

So, the numerator and denominator increase by 4 each time.

$$\frac{13 + 4}{16 + 4} = \frac{17}{20}$$

26) The correct answer is D. For questions about distance like this one, keep in mind that the locations may or may not lie on a straight line. For example, the locations could be laid out like this:

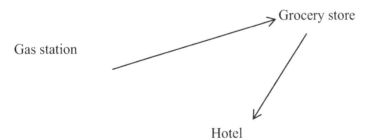

In the layout above, the gas station would be 16 miles from the hotel.

However, the locations could also be laid out like this:

Grocery store

Gas station

Hotel

We can see that the locations will be the farthest from each other if they are laid out on a straight line as in the first example above. In other words, a person could always go to the hotel by traveling to the grocery store from the gas station (10 miles) and then traveling from the grocery store to the hotel (6 miles). Therefore, the gas station would never be more than 16 miles away from the hotel, regardless of the layout.

27) The correct answer is A. The perimeter of a rectangle is equal to two times the length plus two times the width. We can express this concept as an equation: P = 2L + 2W. Now set up formulas for the perimeters both before and after the increase.

Before the increase:
P = 2L + 2W
48 = 2L + 2W
48 ÷ 2 = (2L + 2W) ÷ 2
24 = L + W
24 – W = L

After the increase (width is increased by 5 and length is doubled):
P = 2L + 2W
92 = (2×2)L + 2(W + 5)
92 = 4L + 2W + 10
92 – 10 = 4L + 2W
82 = 4L + 2W

Then solve by substitution. In this case, we substitute 24 – W (which we calculated in the before" equation in step 1) for L in the "after" equation calculated in step 2, in order to solve for W.
82 = 4L + 2W
82 = 4(24 – W) + 2W
82 = 96 – 4W + 2W
82 – 96 = 96 – 96 – 4W + 2W
–14 = –2W
7 = W

Then substitute the value for W in order to solve for L.
24 – W = L
24 – 7 = L
17 = L

28) The correct answer is C. From the formulas provided, we can see that cos A = sin (90° – A). If sin B = cos A, as in this problem, then sin B = sin (90° – 42°) = sin 48° = sin B. A = 42° and B = 48°, so A + B = 90°

29) The correct answer is B. Our facts were: 5 more than 4 times the number x is equal to the number y minus the number z. Build up your equation based on each part of the problem.
4 times the number x: $4x$
5 more than 4 times the number x: $4x + 5$
5 more than 4 times the number x is equal to the number y: $4x + 5 = y$
5 more than 4 times the number x is equal to the number y minus the number z: $4x + 5 = y - z$

30) The correct answer is D. The base length of the triangle described in the problem, which is line segment BC, is not given. So, we need to calculate the base length using the Pythagorean theorem. According to the Pythagorean theorem, the length of the hypotenuse is equal to the square root of the sum of the squares of the two other sides.

$$\sqrt{A^2 + B^2} = C$$

$$\sqrt{6^2 + B^2} = 9$$

$$\sqrt{36 + B^2} = 9$$

Now square each side of the equation in order to solve for the base length.

$$\sqrt{36 + B^2} = 9$$

$$\left(\sqrt{36 + B^2}\right)^2 = 9^2$$

$$36 + B^2 = 81$$

$$36 - 36 + B^2 = 81 - 36$$

$$B^2 = 45$$

$$\sqrt{B^2} = \sqrt{45}$$

$$\sqrt{B^2} = \sqrt{9 \times 5}$$

$$\sqrt{B^2} = \sqrt{3^2 \times 5}$$

$$B = 3\sqrt{5}$$

Now solve for the area of the triangle.

triangle area = (base × height) ÷ 2

$$\left(3\sqrt{5} \times 6\right) \div 2$$

31) The correct answer is A. For these problems, remember that to increase the output of y, we need to increase the input of x. Likewise, to increase the output of x, we need to increase the input of y. If the curve is stretched vertically by 3, this affects the output of y, so we need to increase the input of x. Accordingly, the new equation thus far becomes: $y = 3x^2$. If the curve is then moved up 2 units, we need to increase the output of y, so we can add 2 to the x side or subtract 2 from the y variable of the new equation, making the equation thus far: $y - 2 = 3x^2$. Shifting the curve 4 units to the right is horizontal shift, meaning that we need to modify x in x^2 to become $(x - 4)^2$. So, our final equation is: $y - 2 = 3(x - 4)^2$.

32) The correct answer is D. The graph is of a quadratic, so the equation must have a variable raised to the power of 2. So, Answer A is incorrect. The parabola is downward facing, so the leading coefficient must be negative. Answer choice D meets this criterion, but answers B and C do not.

Further, we can identify points (0, 10) and (5, –15) from the graph. So, we can check the answer as follows:

$f(x) = -(x^2) + 10$

$f(x) = -(0^2) + 10 = 10$

$f(x) = -(x^2) + 10$

$f(x) = -(5^2) + 10 = -25 + 10 = -15$

Since the coordinates on the graph satisfy equation D, it is the correct answer.

33) The correct answer is A. Calculate the area of the triangle: $\frac{1}{2} \times base \times height = \frac{1}{2} \times 5 \times 6 = \frac{1}{2} \times 30 = 15$. The height of the unshaded part is 9 inches since $15 - 6 = 9$, so next we can calculate the area of the unshaded rectangular part: base × height = $5 \times 9 = 45$. Add the area of the unshaded part of the figure to the area of the triangle in order to get the area for the entire figure: $45 + 15 = 60$. Finally, express the result as a simplified fraction with the area of the triangle in the numerator and the area of the entire figure in the denominator: $^{15}/_{60} = ^{1}/_{4}$

34) The correct answer is C. Consider the communicative, associate, and distributive properties when you are analyzing each of the answer choices. Statement I is true because of the communicative property of multiplication. In other words, $x \times y = y \times x$. Statement IV is true because y is a positive number and z, as a subtracted number, is the last operation to be performed on both sides of the equation.

35) The correct answer is D. The two angles are congruent since the two lines intersect in the center of the rectangle.

36) The correct answer is D. We want to calculate the length of side BC, which is the opposite side of this triangle. We have the length of the hypotenuse, so we can determine the length of side BC as follows:

sin A = $^{BC}/_{AC}$ ("opposite over hypotenuse")

sin A = $^{BC}/_{14}$

$0.8192 = ^{BC}/_{14}$

$0.8192 \times 14 = BC$

$11.469 = BC$

37) The correct answer is A. tan A = sin A ÷ cos A, so substitute the values into the appropriate formula.

tan A = sin A ÷ cos A

tan A = $0.788 \div 0.616$

tan A = 1.279

38) The correct answer is D. The altitude in the original triangle forms a side of each of the two right triangles that are created when drawing the altitude. So, each of these right triangles has one side that is 3 feet long. We will call this side B. Half of the base of the triangle forms another side of

each of these right triangles. So, each of these right triangles has another side that is 1 foot long ($2 \div 2 = 1$). We will call this side A. So, we need to calculate the hypotenuse of these right triangles.

hypotenuse length = $\sqrt{A^2 + B^2}$
$\sqrt{1^2 + 3^2} =$
$\sqrt{1 + 9} = \sqrt{10}$

The kite is formed of these 4 "hypotenuse" edges, so the perimeter is $4\sqrt{10}$.

39) The correct answer is B. Answer A is incorrect because it has x^2, which will be a parabola when graphed. Answer C is incorrect since the slope will be negative, and the line will decline from left to right. Answer D is incorrect because the equation has an absolute value. The graph shows a straight line so, the equation must be in the form $y = mx + b$. So, B is the correct answer.

40) The correct answer is C. The volume of a cuboid is: length × width × height

The length is 16 cm and the width is 14 cm, so put in the values and work the formula in reverse to find the height:
2,016 = 16 × 14 × height
2,016 ÷ 16 ÷ 14 = height
9 = height

The length width and height are each increased by 20%, so find the new measurements:
length = 16 × 1.20 = 19.2
width = 14 × 1.20 = 16.8
height = 9 × 1.20 = 10.8

Then multiply these three amounts together to get the volume of the enlarged cuboid:
19.2 × 16.8 × 10.8 = 3483.648

Answers to Classic Learning Test Practice Math Exam 5

1) The correct answer is D. The factors of 50 are: $1 \times 50 = 50$; $2 \times 25 = 50$; $5 \times 10 = 50$. If any of your factors are perfect squares, you can simplify the radical. 25 is a perfect square, so, you need to factor inside the radical sign as shown to solve the problem: $\sqrt{50} = \sqrt{25 \times 2} = \sqrt{5^2 \times 2} = \sqrt{5^2} \times \sqrt{2} = 5\sqrt{2}$

2) The correct answer is D. 36 is the common factor, So, factor the amounts inside the radicals and simplify: $\sqrt{36} + 4\sqrt{72} - 2\sqrt{144} = \sqrt{36} + 4\sqrt{36 \times 2} - 2\sqrt{36 \times 4} = \sqrt{6 \times 6} + 4\sqrt{(6 \times 6) \times 2} - 2\sqrt{(6 \times 6) \times 4} = 6 + (4 \times 6)\sqrt{2} - (2 \times 6)\sqrt{4} = 6 + 24\sqrt{2} - (12 \times 2) = 6 + 24\sqrt{2} - 24 = -18 + 24\sqrt{2}$

3) The correct answer is A. $\sqrt{7} \times \sqrt{11} = \sqrt{7 \times 11} = \sqrt{77}$

4) The correct answer is B. The cube root is the number which satisfies the equation when multiplied by itself two times: $\sqrt[3]{\dfrac{216}{27}} = \sqrt[3]{\dfrac{6 \times 6 \times 6}{3 \times 3 \times 3}} = \dfrac{6}{3} = 2$

5) The correct answer is A. The base number is 7. Since the base number is the same on both terms, we can add the exponents: $7^5 \times 7^3 = 7^{(5+3)} = 7^8$

6) The correct answer is B. The base is xy. Since the base variable is the same on both terms, we can subtract the exponents: $(xy)^6 \div (xy)^3 = (xy)^{(6-3)} = (xy)^3$

7) The correct answer is D. When you have a fraction as an exponent, the numerator is new exponent and the denominator goes in front as the root: $\sqrt{x^{\frac{5}{7}}} = \left(\sqrt[7]{x}\right)^5$

8) The correct answer is B. $x^{-5} = \dfrac{1}{x^5}$

9) The correct answer is C. We have a non-zero number raised to the power of zero, so it is equal to 1.

10) The correct answer is C. When you divide by a fraction, invert the fraction and multiply.
$$\dfrac{b + \frac{2}{7}}{\frac{1}{b}} = \left(b + \dfrac{2}{7}\right) \div \dfrac{1}{b} = \left(b + \dfrac{2}{7}\right) \times \dfrac{b}{1} = b\left(b + \dfrac{2}{7}\right) = b^2 + \dfrac{2b}{7}$$

11) The correct answer is D. Find the lowest common denominator for the second fraction by multiplying it by $x + 2$. Then add the numerators.
$$\dfrac{x^2}{x^2 + 2x} + \dfrac{8}{x} = \dfrac{x^2}{x^2 + 2x} + \left(\dfrac{8}{x} \times \dfrac{x + 2}{x + 2}\right) = \dfrac{x^2}{x^2 + 2x} + \dfrac{8x + 16}{x^2 + 2x} = \dfrac{x^2 + 8x + 16}{x^2 + 2x}$$

12) The correct answer is A. Multiply as shown:

$$\frac{2a^3}{7} \times \frac{3}{a^2} = \frac{2a^3 \times 3}{7 \times a^2} = \frac{6a^3}{7a^2}$$

Then find the greatest common factor and cancel out to simplify:

$$\frac{6a^3}{7a^2} = \frac{6a \times a^2}{7 \times a^2} = \frac{6a \times \cancel{a^2}}{7 \times \cancel{a^2}} = \frac{6a}{7}$$

13) The correct answer is B. Invert and multiply.

$$\frac{8x + 8}{x^4} \div \frac{5x + 5}{x^2} =$$

$$\frac{8x + 8}{x^4} \times \frac{x^2}{5x + 5} =$$

$$\frac{(8x \times x^2) + (8 \times x^2)}{(x^4 \times 5x) + (x^4 \times 5)} =$$

$$\frac{8x^3 + 8x^2}{5x^5 + 5x^4}$$

Then factor out $(x + 1)$ from the numerator and denominator and cancel out:

$$\frac{8x^3 + 8x^2}{5x^5 + 5x^4} =$$

$$\frac{(8x^2 \times x) + (8x^2 \times 1)}{(5x^4 \times x) + (5x^4 \times 1)} =$$

$$\frac{8x^2(x + 1)}{5x^4(x + 1)} =$$

$$\frac{8x^2\cancel{(x + 1)}}{5x^4\cancel{(x + 1)}} =$$

$$\frac{8x^2}{5x^4}$$

Finally, factor out x^2 and cancel it out:

$$\frac{8x^2}{5x^4} =$$

$$\frac{x^2 \times 8}{x^2 \times 5x^2} =$$

$$\frac{\cancel{x^2} \times 8}{\cancel{x^2} \times 5x^2} =$$

$$\frac{8}{5x^2}$$

14) The correct answer is D. Use the FOIL method to expand the polynomial.

FIRST – Multiply the first term from the first set of parentheses by the first term from the second set of parentheses: $(\boldsymbol{x} + 4y)(\boldsymbol{x} + 4y) = x \times x = x^2$

OUTSIDE – Multiply the first term from the first set of parentheses by the second term from the second set of parentheses: $(\boldsymbol{x} + 4y)(x + \boldsymbol{4y}) = x \times 4y = 4xy$

INSIDE – Multiply the second term from the first set of parentheses by the first term from the second set of parentheses: $(x + \boldsymbol{4y})(\boldsymbol{x} + 4y) = 4y \times x = 4xy$

LAST– Multiply the second term from the first set of parentheses by the second term from the second set of parentheses: $(x + \boldsymbol{4y})(x + \boldsymbol{4y}) = 4y \times 4y = 16y^2$

Finally, we add all of the products together: $x^2 + 4xy + 4xy + 16y^2 = x^2 + 8xy + 16y^2$

15) The correct answer is B. The numerator remains the same on each fraction, but the denominator increases by 5 each time. So, 1/26 is the next number.

16) The correct answer is D. If a term or variable is subtracted within the parentheses, you have to keep the negative sign with it when you multiply.

FIRST: $(\boldsymbol{x} - y)(\boldsymbol{x} + y) = x \times x = x^2$

OUTSIDE: $(\boldsymbol{x} - y)(x + \boldsymbol{y}) = x \times y = xy$

INSIDE: $(x - \boldsymbol{y})(\boldsymbol{x} + y) = -y \times x = -xy$

LAST: $(x - \boldsymbol{y})(x + \boldsymbol{y}) = -y \times y = -y^2$

SOLUTION: $x^2 + xy + - xy - y^2 = x^2 - y^2$

17) The correct answer is A. First, Isolate the whole numbers.

$50 - \frac{3x}{5} \geq 41$

$- \frac{3x}{5} \geq 41 - 50$

$- \frac{3x}{5} \geq -9$

Then get rid of the denominator on the fraction.

$- \frac{3x}{5} \geq -9$

$\left(5 \times - \frac{3x}{5}\right) \geq -9 \times 5$

$-3x \geq -9 \times 5$

$-3x \geq -45$

Then isolate the remaining whole numbers.

$-3x \geq -45$

$-3x \div 3 \geq -45 \div 3$

$-x \geq -15$

Then deal with the negative number.

$-x \geq -15$

$-x + 15 \geq -15 + 15$

$-x + 15 \geq 0$

Finally, isolate the unknown variable as a positive number.
$-x + 15 \geq 0$
$-x + x + 15 \geq 0 + x$
$15 \geq x$
$x \leq 15$

18) The correct answer is D. Substitute values as shown: $x - 2 > 5$ and $y = x - 2$, so $y > 5$. If two wizfits are being purchased, we need to solve for $2y$:
$y \times 2 > 5 \times 2$
$2y > 10$

19) The correct answer is B. For quadratic inequality problems like this one, you need to factor the inequality first. The factors of -9 are: -1×9; -3×3; 1×-9. We do not have a term with only the x variable, so we need factors that add up to zero, so factor as shown:
$x^2 - 9 < 0$
$(x + 3)(x - 3) < 0$

Then find values for x by solving each parenthetical for 0.
$(x + 3) = 0$
$(-3 + 3) = 0$
$x = -3$

$(x - 3) = 0$
$(3 - 3) = 0$
$x = 3$

So, $x > -3$ and $x < 3$. You can then check your work to be sure that you have the inequality signs pointing the right way.

Use -2 to check $x > -3$. Since $-2 > -3$ is correct, our proof should also be correct:
$x^2 - 9 < 0$
$-2^2 - 9 < 0$
$4 - 9 < 0$
$-5 < 0$ (CORRECT)

Use 4 to check for $x < 3$. Since $4 < 3$ is incorrect, our proof should also be incorrect.
$x^2 - 9 < 0$
$4^2 - 9 < 0$
$16 - 9 < 0$
$7 < 0$ (INCORRECT)

Therefore, we have checked that $x > -3$ and $x < 3$.

20) The correct answer is D. We know that the products of 12 are: $1 \times 12 = 12$; $2 \times 6 = 12$; $3 \times 4 = 12$. So, add each of the two factors together to solve the first equation: $1 + 12 = 13$; $2 + 6 = 8$; $3 + 4 = 7$. $(3, 4)$ solves both equations, so it is the correct answer.

21) The correct answer is C. The first term of the second equation is x. To eliminate the x variable, we need to multiply the second equation by 3 because the first equation contains $3x$.

$x + 2y = 8$
$(3 \times x) + (3 \times 2y) = (3 \times 8)$
$3x + 6y = 24$

Now subtract the new second equation from the original first equation.
$$\begin{aligned} 3x + 3y &= 15 \\ -(3x + 6y &= 24) \\ \hline -3y &= -9 \end{aligned}$$

Then solve for y.
$-3y = -9$
$-3y \div -3 = -9 \div -3$
$y = 3$

Using our original second equation of $x + 2y = 8$, substitute the value of 3 for y to solve for x.
$x + 2y = 8$
$x + (2 \times 3) = 8$
$x + 6 = 8$
$x = 8 - 6$
$x = 2$

22) The correct answer is D. Substitute values for $x = 2$ and $y = 4$ to solve:
$\frac{x^4}{y^2} - 6 = \frac{2^4}{4^2} - 6 = \frac{16}{16} - 6 = -5$

23) The correct answer is C. Deduct the degrees provided for angle A from 180° to find out the total degrees of the two other angles: $180° - 32° = 148°$. Since this is an isosceles triangle, the remaining two angles have the same measurement. So, divide by two in order to find out how many degrees each angle has: $148° \div 2 = 74°$

24) The correct answer is B. The angle given in the problem is 90°. If we divide the total of 360° in the circle by the 90° angle, we have: $360 \div 90 = 4$. You can think of arc length as the partial circumference of a circle, so we can visualize that there are 4 such arcs along this circle. We can then multiply the number of arcs by the length of each arc to get the circumference of the circle: $4 \times 8\pi = 32\pi$ (circumference). Finally, use the formula for the circumference of the circle to solve.
Circumference = $\pi \times$ radius $\times 2$
$32\pi = \pi \times 2 \times$ radius
$32\pi \div 2 = \pi \times$ radius
$16\pi = \pi \times$ radius
$16 =$ radius

25) The correct answer is D. The area of a rectangle is equal to its length times its width. The field is 32 yards wide and 100 yards long, so now we can substitute the values.
rectangle area = width × length
rectangle area = 32×100
rectangle area = 3200

26) The correct answer is A. Substitute the value of the diameter into the formula:
circumference = D × π = 6π

27) The correct answer is D. The center of this circle is (−5, 5) and the point of tangency is (−5, 0).
We need to subtract these two coordinates in order to find the length of the radius:
(−5, 5) − (−5, 0) = (0, 5). In other words, the radius length is 5, so the diameter length is 10.

28) The correct answer is C. The base length of the triangle described in the problem, which is $\overline{YZ}$, is
not given. So, we need to calculate the base length using the Pythagorean theorem. According to
the Pythagorean theorem, the length of the hypotenuse is equal to the square root of the sum of
the squares of the two other sides.

$\sqrt{A^2 + B^2} = C$
$\sqrt{4^2 + B^2} = 5$
$\sqrt{16 + B^2} = 5$

Now square each side of the equation in order to solve for the base length.
$\sqrt{16 + B^2} = 5$
$\left(\sqrt{16 + B^2}\right)^2 = 5^2$
$16 + B^2 = 25$
$B^2 = 25 − 16$
$B^2 = 9$
$\sqrt{B^2} = \sqrt{9}$
$B = 3$

Now solve for the area of the triangle.
triangle area = (base × height) ÷ 2
triangle area = (3 × 4) ÷ 2
triangle area = 12 ÷ 2
triangle area = 6

29) The correct answer is D. Triangle XYZ is a 30°–60°–90° triangle. Using the Pythagorean
theorem, its sides are therefore in the ratio of 1: $\sqrt{3}$: 2. Using relative measurements, the line
segment opposite the 30° angle is 1 unit long, the line segment opposite the 60° angle is $\sqrt{3}$ units
long, and the line segment opposite the right angle (the hypotenuse) is 2 units long. In this
problem, line segment XY is opposite the 30° angle, so it is 1 proportional unit long. Line
segment YZ is opposite the 60° angle, so it is $\sqrt{3}$ proportional units long. Line segment XZ (the
hypotenuse) is the line opposite the right angle, so it is 2 proportional units long. So, in order to
keep the measurements in proportion, we need to set up the following proportion: $\frac{XY}{YZ} = \frac{1}{\sqrt{3}}$. Now
substitute the known measurement of YZ from the figure, which is 5 in this problem.

$$\frac{XY}{YZ} = \frac{1}{\sqrt{3}}$$

$$\frac{XY}{5} = \frac{1}{\sqrt{3}}$$

$$\left(\frac{XY}{5} \times 5\right) = \left(\frac{1}{\sqrt{3}} \times 5\right)$$

$$XY = \frac{5}{\sqrt{3}}$$

30) The correct answer is C. Write out the formula: (length × 2) + (width × 2). Then substitute the values. (17 × 2) + (4 × 2) = 34 + 8 = 42

31) The correct answer is C. A radian is the measurement of an angle at the center of a circle which is subtended by an arc that is equal in length to the radius of the circle. We need to use the formula to calculate the length of the arc: s = r θ. Substitute values to solve the problem.
radius (r) = 4
radians (θ) = $^\pi/_4$
s = r θ
s = 4 × $^\pi/_4$
s = π

32) The correct answer is C. Substitute the values from the problem into the formula provided.
cone volume = [height × radius^2 × π] ÷ 3
cone volume = [9 × 4^2 × π] ÷ 3
cone volume = [9 × 16 × π] ÷ 3
cone volume = 144π ÷ 3
cone volume = 48π

33) The correct answer is B. First, find the midpoint of the *x* coordinates for (**−4**, 2) and (**8**,−6).
midpoint $x = (x_1 + x_2) ÷ 2$
midpoint $x = (−4 + 8) ÷ 2$
midpoint $x = 4 ÷ 2$
midpoint $x = 2$

Then find the midpoint of the *y* coordinates for (−4, **2**) and (8,**−6**).
midpoint $y = (y_1 + y_2) ÷ 2$
midpoint $y = (2 + −6) ÷ 2$
midpoint $y = −4 ÷ 2$
midpoint $y = −2$
So, the midpoint is (2, −2)

34) The correct answer is A. Substitute the values into the slope-intercept formula.
The slope-intercept formula is $y = mx + b$, where m is the slope and b is the y-intercept.
$y = mx + b$
$315 = m5 + 15$
$315 - 15 = m5$
$300 = m5$
$300 \div 5 = m5 \div 5$
$60 = m$

35) The correct answer is A. The x intercept is the point at which a line crosses the x axis of a graph. In order for the line to cross the x axis, y must be equal to zero at that particular point of the graph. On the other hand, the y intercept is the point at which the line crosses the y axis. So, in order for the line to cross the y axis, x must be equal to zero at that particular point of the graph.

First, substitute 0 for y in order to find the x intercept.
$x^2 + 2y^2 = 144$
$x^2 + (2 \times 0) = 144$
$x^2 + 0 = 144$
$x^2 = 144$
$x = 12$

Then substitute 0 for x in order to find the y intercept.
$x^2 + 2y^2 = 144$
$(0 \times 0) + 2y^2 = 144$
$0 + 2y^2 = 144$
$2y^2 \div 2 = 144 \div 2$
$y^2 = 72$
$y = \sqrt{72}$
So, the y intercept is $(0, \sqrt{72})$ and the x intercept is $(12, 0)$.

36) The correct answer is D. You will recall from the formulas that $\sin A = \cos(90° - A)$.
If $\sin B = \cos A$, as in this problem, then $B = 90° - A$ and $A + B = 90°$

37) The correct answer is C. Since the greatest possible value of cosine is 1, $\cos 2x$ must be less than or equal to 1. So, the greatest possible value of $\cos 2x$ is represented by the following formula: $\cos 2x = 1$. Now, multiply each side of the equation by 4 in order to get $4 \times \cos 2x$.
$\cos 2x = 1$
$4 \times \cos 2x = 1 \times 4$
$4 \times \cos 2x = 4$
So, the greatest possible value is 4.

38) The correct answer is A. $\sin^2$ of any angle is always equal to $1 - \cos^2$ of that angle.

39) The correct answer is C. From the trigonometric formulas, we know that $\cos A = \frac{y}{z}$ (adjacent over hypotenuse) and $\tan A = \frac{x}{y}$ (opposite over adjacent).

For our problem $\cos A = \frac{9}{15}$ so the adjacent side is $y = 9$ and the hypotenuse $z = 15$. $\tan A = \frac{12}{9}$ so the opposite side $x = 12$ and again $y = 9$.

Now substitute the values for sine. For our problem, the opposite side $x = 12$ and the hypotenuse $z = 15$. $\sin A = \frac{x}{z} = \frac{opposite}{hypotenuse}$, so for our question, $\sin A = \frac{12}{15}$.

40) The correct answer is C. Substitute the value of $x = 2$ to solve: $5^x = 5^2 = 25$

Made in United States
Orlando, FL
19 July 2023

35280573R00070